W9-BSV-348

Once Upon a Time in Asia

Stories of Harmony and Peace

Once Upon a Time in Asia

Stories of Harmony and Peace

Compiled by James H. Kroeger
and
Eugene F. Thalman

ORBIS BOOKS
Maryknoll, New York 10545

Founded in 1970, Orbis Books endeavors to publish works that enlighten the mind, nourish the spirit, and challenge the conscience. The publishing arm of the Maryknoll Fathers and Brothers, Orbis seeks to explore the global dimensions of the Christian faith and mission, to invite dialogue with diverse cultures and religious traditions, and to serve the cause of reconciliation and peace. The books published reflect the views of their authors and do not represent the official position of the Maryknoll Society. To learn more about Maryknoll and Orbis Books, please visit our website at www.maryknoll.org.

Published by Orbis Books, Maryknoll, New York 10545-0308.
Manufactured in the United States of America.

Library of Congress Cataloging-in-Publication Data

Once upon a time in Asia : stories of harmony and peace / compiled by James H. Kroeger and Eugene F. Thalman.
     p. cm.
  ISBN-13: 978-1-57075-637-5 (pbk.)
  1. Asia—Religion. 2. Mythology, Asian. 3. Folklore—Asia. 4. Folk literature. I. Kroeger, James H. II. Thalman, Eugene F.
  BL1033.O53 2006
  200.95—dc22
                              2006009469

ISBN 1-57075-686-4

In memory of Eugene F. Thalman, M.M.
(1933–2005)

Contents

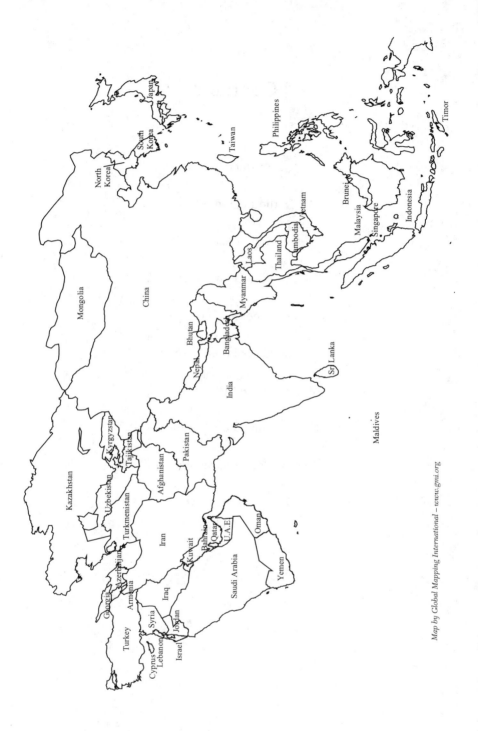

Map by Global Mapping International – www.gmi.org

Introduction

The world is full of stories. We are familiar with their telling and re-telling. A simple introduction can alert us: "And so it happened that..." or "Once upon a time..." or "In the past when...." Spontaneously, our ears, minds, and hearts become attentive. We listen to the narratives and search for their meaning. And in Asia, with its many literary treasures, stories from the past, preserved as history, shape contemporary lives, which, in turn, create new stories.

Stories tell us who we are and they also link us with other people, in Asia and throughout the world. They help us explore the deeper dimensions of life and the mystery of our own being. Stories possess tremendous power as they impact our life and our faith.

Stories also help define and sustain individuals, families, communities, and indeed, nations. They open a window through which we can view the world, perceiving meaning and gaining insight. Stories capture the human experience, telling of joy, peace, grace, forgiveness, compassion, conversion, reconciliation, and unity. They probe deeply into the human heart, into life's mysteries, and into human relationships with God and others. Stories emerging from the rich traditions of Asia can shed light on our common spiritual journey, whether we are Hindu, Muslim, Buddhist, or Christian. Together we are all on a spiritual pilgrimage.

Without doubt, people remember stories long after they may have forgotten the lessons they learned in school or the books they read. It is little wonder then that across ages and cultures, grandparents and sages, preachers and teachers have enthralled and challenged their listeners with stories. One striking example is Jesus, a master-teacher (*rabbi*) who used parables to present us with new possibilities in our relations with God and all our brothers and sisters. Like the great wisdom teachers of Asia, such as Confucius, Lao Tzu, Chuang Tzu, or Gandhi, Jesus gathered up experiences and anecdotes from daily life, inviting us to see life with new eyes and to open our arms and hearts to those around us.

The narratives in this collection include a variety of forms: Asian oral and written literature, poems, prayers, experiences, myths, and fiction. Also, pay close attention to the stories told through the art that accompanies the printed word. Be inspired, take a moment for reflection, laugh or shed a tear, discover your deeper self. Hopefully, your own personal story and song will resonate with the narratives and melodies of all God's peoples in Asia.

I sincerely wish to thank the scores of generous people who contributed material for this volume, including those persons whose stories were not used as well as those contributors whose names are mentioned after the texts. I want to acknowledge the good work done by Father Eugene F. Thalman, M.M., who initiated the project before his untimely death. And special thanks are due to Jason K. Dy, S.J., the young Filipino-Chinese artist whose drawings enhance the book, and to Susan Perry, the Orbis Books editor and friend who marvelously guided the project with such great skill and dedication. Sincere thanks— our stories have become forever intertwined.

James H. Kroeger, M.M.
Manila, Philippines
March 25, 2006

In the Beginning

"Life can be found only in the present moment."
Thich Nhat Hanh

Asia's peoples, in all their rich diversity, have reflected deeply on the origins of life, expressing their insights in unique myths and stories—like almost all cultures known throughout history. A clear reverence for the mystery and beauty of life emerges. The origins of life—the earth and the heavens, plants and animals, all living things and especially the human family—are linked with the divine. Life is a gift, an awesome, precious treasure.

Asia's genesis stories and myths also reflect upon the human quest for happiness. Everyone's experience of life is shaped by temptation, sin, and evil, which can make happiness seem illusive, but virtue and good are also profound influences. This is part of the human journey.

Like most myths, those of Asia are not primitive, naïve understandings. Rather, they contain profound insights, insights that could never be achieved by scientific description or logical analysis. In this spirit, take a journey with some of Asia's peoples. Discover God's marvelous gift of life.

The Story of Creation

In the beginning, there was only the sea. Floating on this sea was a thing resembling a ball, which was the abode of God the Most High. When God was ready, the ball split. One half of it rose and became heaven and the lower half remained and became the earth. The part of the ball that remained was the mother, and the part that was lifted up was the father, and the sea on which it floated was the grandfather. Now, at the time of the splitting of the ball, and as God willed it, all people and all the creatures on earth were already in it but not released. From the time of our ancestors up to the present, the original content is what we have been looking for.

When Allah the Most High was in the highest heaven, his radiance scattered and became a man, Nur (meaning "light") Muhammad. Now when Nur Muhammad became aware of himself, he asserted that he was God. Looking left and right, he saw that he was alone and said to himself, "There is nobody but me, so I must be God." He then announced, "*Arastrum Murabbikim*," meaning "I am God." All of a sudden, a voice answered "*Kahal Bala*," and Nur disintegrated.

When this happened, all the elements contained in the earth and the heavens were drawn out of him. From the single light of Nur came the moon, the sun, the stars, the trees, and all living things. They were all there. This was begun on a Sunday and was completed on a Friday.

After all things had been drawn out of Nur Muhammad, he was made man once again and God said to him, "Do not assert that you are God. I am God. But if you do not believe this, let us play hide and seek. You hide and I will look for you. Then I will hide and you look for me. If I can find you and you cannot find me, them surely I am God." And so they commenced the game. No matter where Nur Muhammad hid, God always located him. Then God said, "Now I will hide," and Nur Muhammad could not find him. (And Hadji Hussin, with a twinkle in his eyes, later explained that this is why we cannot see God.)

Then God said to Jibra'il (Gabriel), "Go down to earth and get a handful of soil." When Jibra'il descended to pick up some earth, the earth cursed and refused to be taken. Jibra'il returned empty-handed, and God said to Mika'il, "You go." When he reached the earth he met the same refusal. Then Isra'il took his turn, but the earth likewise refused. Then the fourth angel, Idjara'il (Iza'il or Azrae'el) immediately went down and forthwith grabbed the earth. One of his fingers was on the west, another on the east, a third one on the south, and a fourth one on the earth. Thus he scooped up a handful of soil.

Then God said to Jibra'il, "Make it into a man." When the earth assumed the form of a man, Jibra'il said to God, "My Lord, the man is here but it cannot speak, and its joints are not connected."

Then God said, "Get a *ganta* of rice and grind it into powder and apply it to him." Then the joints were connected and the man became whole, but he still could not speak. Then God commanded Nur Muhammad, "Go inside Adam" (for that was the name of the man). But Nur Muhammad said, "I refuse. You created Adam from the four elements of fire, water, wind, and earth, whereas I came from your light." Then God said to Nur Muhammad, "Be willing, for you and I are one, and you can meet me five times a day during prayer." So Nur Muhammad went inside Adam through his forehead and Adam became a living man.

And God made Adam into a caliph and commanded all creatures, including the angels, to pay homage to him. And every creature did, except Iblis (the Evil One) who said to God, "How can I worship Adam, seeing that he was created out of four elements, whereas I have served you for hundreds of years?" In spite of God's entreaty, Iblis continued to refuse.

Then Iblis asked God to grant him four wishes. First, that he would be the richest of all; second, that he would be most exalted of all; third, that he could steal the riches of those who have; and fourth, that those whose riches he could not steal, he would kill. And this is the origin of the evil desire for material goods and for worldly fame that leads to envy and killing. Those whom Iblis enters into are led into evil, for Iblis had an agreement with God that those he could mislead would be his and those he could not would be God's.

A Samal folk epic from the Philippines,
adapted from Filipino Heritage 1
(Singapore: Lahing Pilipino Publishing, Inc., 1977)
Father James H. Kroeger, M.M., Manila, Philippines

The Peacock and the Mustard Garden

In the beginning when God created the heavens and the earth, the thirty creations lived happily on the earth. God created nine families in heaven and seven families on the earth. The human beings and animals and all of creation understood one language and everything worked in peace and harmony.

The Princess Sun and the Prince Peacock were happily married and had duties to fulfill. The Princess Sun ruled the heavens and the earth and was responsible for seeing that the heavens and the whole of the universe worked in harmony and that the earth got sunshine.

One day the Peacock, sitting idle, chanced to look down on the earth. He was so captivated by a beautiful lady with masses of golden hair spreading over the land that he could neither eat nor sleep. Princess Sun worried about the change in her beloved husband, and when she learned that he had fallen in love with a lady on the earth, she pleaded with him to stay calm. But the Peacock did not listen to his wife the Sun. Although the Princess Sun was heartbroken, she graciously allowed her husband to go, knowing that he could never return to her.

The Peacock left and the Sun's tears flickered in the sunlight as they dropped down on his feathers. The Peacock reached the earth and, to his disappointment, the golden lady who had attracted him was nothing but a field of mustard. He wept and flapped his wings to fly back to his beloved wife, but he could not rise high enough. To this day, the Peacock flaps his wings when it rains while the sun is shining.

Adapted from Khasi folklore, Silvia Ines, Northeast India

The Sun and the Moon

A long time ago, there were two suns and it was very, very hot. All the creatures on the planet complained about the heat. One day a meeting was held and one of the creatures suggested getting rid of one of the suns. Without hesitation, everyone agreed.

But the question was, who would be in charge of the job and how was it to be done? The task fell to the ant, who was famous for his good aim. Well, the poor little ant went out in the heat day after day and at last he shot one of the suns. To everyone's great sadness, however, both suns disappeared and the whole universe became completely dark. Grief rather than happiness overwhelmed all the creatures.

All the creatures realized that they could do nothing without the light of the suns. What should they do? They knew that they had made a great mistake by asking the ant to shoot one of the suns, so they held another meeting. The discussion on how to bring back the suns went on and on for days. At last, they decided to ask a man to go and ask the suns for pardon and beg them to come back. With great hope, the man went, but he met with failure. Next, they asked a crow to go, but the result was the same. Then they tried other creatures, but all of them failed.

Finally, they thought they had a good idea. It occurred to them that the suns might be asleep so they decided to ask the roosters to crow to wake up the suns. Thus, all the roosters crowed and then stopped for a while to see what would happen. Because nothing happened, they crowed for the second time, still with great hope. Then they stopped.

Gradually, though, they began to sense a little warmth and light, so they crowed for a third time. Then, to the surprise of all, back came one sun. All the happy creatures celebrated the success of the roosters. They were even happier when they realized there was only one sun. The one that had been shot had been blinded.

This is why roosters crow three times before the sun rises. The blind sun is now known as the moon.

Folk tale, Francis Htjaru, Myanmar

King Crab

Once upon a time the crab was king. All the small creatures and insects that lived near him were under his rule. As crabs always do, he lived in a country that had many ponds and swamps.

King Crab was a harsh ruler who made laws that the other creatures did not like to keep. One of them was that when he was asleep his subjects should all keep quiet.

One day when the king was sleeping the frogs croaked and laughed so loudly that they woke him. He sent for them and asked them why they had laughed.

"We laughed because the water turtle looked so funny as he crawled along with his house on his back," they answered.

King Crab called for the turtle. "Why do you carry your house on your back?" he asked.

"I carry it on my back," replied the turtle, "because the firefly carries fire with him. I am afraid that he might set fire to my house when I am away from it."

The king sent for the firefly. When he was asked why he carried fire with him, the firefly answered: "The mosquito is a troublesome fellow. He buzzes around and stings me whenever he gets a chance. I carry fire with me so that I can protect myself from him."

Then King Crab called for the mosquito. "Why do you sting the firefly?" asked the king.

The mosquito did not answer, but flew straight toward the king and stung him on the forehead. The king slapped his forehead and killed the mosquito.

When the other mosquitoes heard of the death of their relative, they set out to find King Crab. The cicada, who was the king's guard, saw them coming from his watch tower in a mangrove tree and beat a warning with his wings. King Crab hurried into a hole in the ground.

The story soon spread among the mosquitoes that King Crab was living somewhere in a small hole. They all rushed around and began to hunt for him.

Have you ever had mosquitoes coming buzzing near your ears? That is because they are still looking in every hole they see, trying to find King Crab.

A Filipino folk tale,
adapted from The Philippines Reader: Book Five
(New York: Ginn & Co., 1947)
Father James H. Kroeger, M.M., Manila, Philippines

Creation Myth from Timor

Many years ago, a small crocodile lived in a faraway place. He dreamed of becoming a big crocodile, but food was scarce. He grew weak.

He decided to leave for the open sea to find food and realize his dream, but the day became increasingly hot and he was still far from the sea. The little crocodile—rapidly drying out and now in desperation—lay down to die.

A little boy took pity on the stranded crocodile and carried him to the sea. Instantly revived, the crocodile said, "Little boy, you have saved my life. If I can ever help you in any way, please call me. I will be at your command."

A few years later the boy called the crocodile, who was now big and strong. "Brother Crocodile," he said. "I too have a dream. I want to see the world."

"Climb on my back," said the crocodile, "and tell me which way to go."

"Follow the sun," said the boy.

The crocodile set off for the east. They traveled the oceans for years, until one day the crocodile said to the boy, "Brother, we have been traveling for a long time. But now the time has come for me to die. In memory of your kindness, I will turn myself into a beautiful island, where you and your children can live until the sun sinks into the sea."

As the crocodile died, he grew and grew, and his ridged back became the mountains, and his scales the hills of Timor.

Sister Theresa Hougnon, M.M., East Timor,
Maryknoll (*May/June 2004*)

Living in Asia

"Fall seven times, rise up eight."
Japanese proverb

Life pulsates throughout the vast Asian continent, home to nearly two-thirds of humanity. The fecundity of Asia is phenomenal: China and India each have populations exceeding one billion. Asia spans ten time zones, and the vastness of the continent overwhelms.

Asians have resiliency, that marvelous ability to move with the ebb and flow of life, the smooth and the rough, the yin-yang of existence. Asian peoples have dreams and aspirations for the basics of life, for happiness, for peace and prosperity. They are also realists who face poverty and sickness, including AIDS, and life's myriad uncertainties. While the twenty-first century is bringing economic growth and modernization to some areas, many Asian people also experience its dark side: the steady erosion of traditional values and, for a large part of the population, increasing poverty and marginalization.

The following narratives give a sampling of life across the wide expanse of Asia, life that is often bittersweet, holding in balance both beauty and tragedy.

First Be, Then Do

It is better to live by being,
By showing forth the Way in ourselves,
Than by piling up thousands of
Mindless activities and speeches.
It is the Way that keeps everything
Centered in the Core, not our own
Plans and actions we consider good deeds.
Through the power of the Way we can muzzle
Our desire to acquire, possess, and control.
Thus does peace come to us quietly
And effortlessly from beyond ourselves.

English translation by Joseph Petulla
The Tao Te Ching and the Christian Way
(Orbis Books, 1998)

Temple of Life

Pisanu had not walked in seven years. A man of thirty-eight, he was confined to his bed and his family did not know how to take care of him. Pisanu's left leg was practically paralyzed and the doctor at the temple thought it impossible that his patient would ever walk again. But Pisanu felt in his heart that he would one day get up and walk.

One day Pisanu looked at me as if to say "I'm ready to walk." He then took my hand and, after we had talked for a while, he decided the time was right. Pisanu was both excited and fearful, but I stayed by him. Once up from the bed, he slowly stood and, to the amazement of all, began taking slow steps with my help and that of a metal walker.

Pisanu now has another dream of one day walking by himself outside on the temple grounds to enjoy the beauty of nature, especially the flowers and trees. That dream may have to wait for a while, as he has since become very sick.

In the time that I have spent serving the needs of people with HIV/AIDS at Wat Prabaat Nampu Temple in Lopburi, Thailand, I am convinced that it is a "temple of life" and not of death. Most people who come to visit us here are saddened to see that many of our people at the hospice are sick and some are dying. What they do not always see is the inner spirit of my Buddhist sisters and brothers here who simply want to live and take care of themselves as best they can. They do not come here to give up on life but to live and make the most of the time left in their lives. Each day that I come to this place there is a sense of joy and hope deep within me that tells me of a new day to be shared together with our people in this temple of life.

True story, Father Mike Bassano, M.M., Bangkok, Thailand

Five Dead Children—A True Account

We went to Quezon City Hall early in the morning with the five small coffins and laid them at the foot of the flagpole. Hundreds of people streamed back and forth past us all day. The children's bodies were already stinking.

We sent word to the mayor that we would stay there until he buried the children, gave the families in-city relocation, and jailed the officials who had authorized the demolition that killed the children. The demolition had been part of a government sidewalk-clearing operation.

The demolition team had known the children were sick with measles—one had just died—and the parents had pleaded with them not to destroy their homes. The team had gone ahead anyway, so the children had spent the night in *karitons* (street pushcarts) and by morning they were dead.

At City Hall we had the support of the crowds and of the media, who stayed nearly all day, interviewing us many times. A mournful bass drum sounded regularly throughout the day to remind the mayor that God was watching and waiting. The mayor finally agreed to our demands. We didn't discuss all the details, since we wanted to bury the children before sunset. That was a mistake, because we didn't get anything in writing.

We went off in a city truck to the Potter's Field. When the truck stopped at red lights we could smell the children's bodies. The age of the youngest was eleven months; that of the oldest was six years. We walked over old graves to the dirtiest, loneliest corner of the cemetery. It was near the wall, where people throw their garbage. The families opened the coffins for the last time, and a crippled girl cried out to her dead sister, "Maria, Maria, why have you gone away? We have so much playing to do." They slid the caskets into niches in the wall and the cemetery workers sealed in the coffins containing the bodies of the children as the sun went down.

In the days that followed we continued negotiating with the mayor. He wasn't hostile, but neither was he apologetic. He promised in-city relocation but he wouldn't say exactly where. He talked of a task force to investigate the demolition, but again the details were vague. All he actually did was bury the dead children.

The mayor was always neatly dressed and smelled of after-shave. The people were worn out, still stunned by the five deaths, but they stayed to continue the demonstration. Some-how they managed to do up their little girls' hair in delicate lit-tle braids and colored ribbons. It made some of us cry to think of the other little girls with their lovely hair resting in graves.

Negotiations continued for several months, until gradually the people lost interest and one by one left the area.

It's still hard to believe that five children were killed by city workers and no compensation was given, nor would any-one be punished, but, despite all our efforts, that is what hap-pened. We always prefer happy endings, but here, in the Philippines among the poor, many incidents end unhappily.

True story, Denis Murphy, Manila, Philippines

Daily Problems

When a stream strikes a hard rock in the water,
It quickly yields and flows on;
Thus to solve the hardened difficulties
Of our lives we also should yield to them
And flow onward, for we can then return
At a better time to reassess our trials.
But this is a most difficult lesson
To learn and live by.

English translation by Joseph Petulla
The Tao Te Ching and the Christian Way
(Orbis Books, 1998)

Utopia

Timor,
a land that sparks memories in my heart.
Conquistador found a land of sandalwood,
UN peacekeepers, war-scarred folk,
neglecting the promising dawn,
enchanting sunset and
charming face.

Burned-out house now shows its faces—
Some newborn, others faded with time.

A nation now,
as seen from faces and hearts still young—
Many promising,
Others etched with mourning,
Children still singing "By the rivers of Babylon."
Who could have guessed?

Belo said Rome and Utopia were not built in a day—
Just a word of consolation, we might say.
But sandalwood no more, no, nor war—
I never know,
Utopia a dream forever more.

Poem by Acácio Angel,
an East Timorese student in Manila, Philippines

The Man behind Genghis Khan

The thirteenth century was the age of the Mongolian empire. Although Genghis Khan is a well-known historical figure, his father Esuhei was considered by his grandson to have been the "founder of the powerful Mongolian empire and the first wise Khan."

Esuhei appreciated courage no matter where it might be found. He was able to appreciate the courage and the skill of his enemies. After he defeated an enemy, he would pardon him. Learning from his father, Genghis Khan turned his defeated enemies into some of his most loyal and trusted warriors.

Adapted from Michael Standaert's "Steppes in Fiction,"
Far Eastern Economic Review
Father Eugene F. Thalman, M.M, Hong Kong

Food Comes First

Labhlu had a fever and his mother, Rabia, took action to relieve him. After borrowing the largest bucket in their neighborhood, she filled it halfway with water. Then she ordered the boy to kneel and position his head over the container. Using the family's tin cup, she scooped up some water and poured it over Labhlu's feverish head. The water ran across his forehead and dripped back into the bucket. Time and again Rabia scooped water to cool the boy's head until, fifteen minutes later, he began to feel better. This was not a cure; it merely offered the boy relief.

Rabia had not used the small sum of money she keeps in a jar to purchase medicine for fever. The fact is that medicine is not a priority in the lives of the poor villagers of Betka. Ask any villager what she or he wishes to use money for and the honest reply will be: first priority—food; second priority—food; and third priority—food. Many will speak of medicine as the last priority—after food, shelter, and clothing—for hunger must be dealt with, whereas inconvenience can be endured.

True story, Father Bob McCahill, M.M., Bangladesh

The Rabbit in the Moon

As a child in New York I was taught to recognize the face of the man in the moon. In Japan, children are taught to see the silhouette of a rabbit. And this is the story of how the rabbit got there.

Once upon a time, a rabbit came upon a man deep in the night forest. He was sitting by a fire, obviously weakened by hunger. There was a grill on the fire, but there was nothing on the grill. There was no food in sight. The rabbit asked the man where his food was and why he was not eating. The man replied that he was old, tired, and no longer able to catch game or even gather greens in the woods. He added that he was so near to the end of his strength that he thought he would not see the dawn.

On hearing this, the rabbit, moved to compassion, stripped himself of his fur, and jumped onto the grill to serve as food for the old man. The man ate the rabbit and lived through that night and for many years after.

That man was the Buddha, and in thanksgiving to the rabbit, he enshrined the spirit of the rabbit in the night moon.

Folk tale, Father John McAuley, M.M., Japan and New York

Unfinished Work

We never finish our work
Here on earth, however good
Everything seems in our lives.
As long as the truth is derided,
As long as people oppress one another,
Prophets are shouted down,
Statesmen are ignored and pushed aside,
We will need to calmly do our work.
We will run to get warm,
Sit in the shade to cool down,
And eventually things will get better.
We hope for the best.

English translation by Joseph Petulla
The Tao Te Ching and the Christian Way
(*Orbis Books, 1998*)

The Tree Kangaroo

Living in the middle of a tropical rainforest in Irian-Jaya, as I do, provides ample opportunity to observe first-hand God's creation in its still nearly unadulterated form.

One day some men from one of the villages up near the foothills brought me a baby kangaroo, whose mother they had killed while hunting. Thinking that raising it might be fun, I took in the helpless creature.

The news spread quickly through the village, and before long two women were standing at my door to see the newest member of their community. As I opened the door, they brushed

past me, scooped up the little fellow from his box, and took him into their arms. They stroked his fine fur and smothered him with kisses. Before long he was resting comfortably on the breast of one of the women, dangling from her neck in a baby sling. The women spent the rest of day parading him through the village for all to see. Toward evening they returned him to his box and left for the night.

Early the next morning I was startled awake by the sobbing of a death dirge. I assumed that someone had died. When I went outside I saw the two women. They had returned with some food for their little friend, only to find him dead in his box. Their sorrow was genuine and their tears were copious, spontaneous, and totally authentic. They wrapped the small body in the finest piece of cloth they could find and buried the baby kangaroo at the edge of the village, wailing lamentations the whole time.

Since then, this incident has provided me with many rich, wonder-filled moments. How does one fathom the depth of people who can fall so deeply in love with one of God's most humble creatures in less than twenty-four hours? I, on the other hand, might have tossed its body either to my dog or into the river.

True story, Father Vince Cole, M.M., Papua, Indonesia

On Ambition

Yen Huei and Tselu were sitting together with Confucius, and Confucius said, "Why don't you each tell me your ambitions in life?"

Tselu replied, "It is my ambition in life to go about with a horse and a carriage and a light fur coat and share them with my good friends until they are all worn out without any regret."

Yen Huei said, "It is my ambition never to show off and never to brag about myself."

Then Tselu said to Confucius, "May I hear what your ambition is?"

And Confucius replied, "It is my ambition that the old people should be able to live in peace, all friends should be loyal, and all young people should love their elders."

Adapted from Linking the World through English II
(Philippines: Diwa Scholastic Press, 2006)
Father James H. Kroeger, M.M., Manila, Philippines

Metro Tears

The young mother's face beamed as she held her week-old baby in her arms. It was clear that this was the joy of her life. The mother's entire world was focused on her newborn. The scene exuded joy, contentment, fulfillment.

"But why were this twenty-something mother and her beautiful baby sitting in such an awful place?" I wondered as I walked by on my way to the metro station. The highway underpass was crowded, with hundreds of people passing by. The air was thick with dust and pollution from the scores of buses,

cars, jeepneys, and trucks clogging the road. This was summer-time, and the heat in tropical Manila was intense.

And yet, there they were. The industrious young mother had a small makeshift table where she displayed cigarettes, candy, chewing gum, and a few bananas. Her meager daily income would be hardly sufficient for the two of them. Life had not given her many choices, so she sold her simple wares in the thick of the crowds, pollution, and heat.

"What will become of this little child?" I thought as I stared at the scene before me. "How many days before the baby will be sick, due to breathing this awful air and living in such conditions?" I was sweating in the few seconds it took me to walk through the underpass, but the mother and baby would be there all day! O, poor baby, what future do you have? Loving mother, I admire your sacrifice to earn something for your new-born. May your sweet baby somehow be saved from sickness and premature death!

My journey on the metro to downtown Manila was uncomfortable, even though I sat in an air-conditioned train. And I couldn't hold back my tears. What price the world's little people pay each day. Often even their simple joys are stolen by sickness and death. Life, so bittersweet.

True story, Father James H. Kroeger, M.M., Manila, Philippines

Bullshit and the Buddha

During the Northern Song dynasty in ancient China, a low-ranking official named Su Shi, who was also a renowned and erudite scholar, was persecuted by some court officials and subsequently exiled to a remote southern county. He was very depressed and disappointed, since his dreams of serving his country and the court wouldn't be achieved.

One day, in an attempt to assuage his depression, someone suggested that he pay a visit to his friend, a Buddhist master with sublime virtue at Hua Yan monastery in the forest. Su Shi decided to do this.

When Su Shi arrived at the monastery, he found the master standing in front of the main gate to welcome him. The two old friends were quite happy to see each other, but very soon the master realized that Mr. Su was very unhappy.

"Are you all right, Mr. Su?" asked the master. "Why are you frowning? Is anything wrong?" Mr. Su did not respond. Knowing from other sources that his visitor might be bemoaning his fate, the master changed the subject.

A little while later, a maid served them green tea. While they were drinking the tea and playing chess, the master asked, "Mr. Su, what do I look like?"

Mr. Su, who decided to take this opportunity to make fun of the master, replied, "Oh, revered master, you look like a pile of ugly bullshit, don't you?" Then he laughed. He thought that the master would be very annoyed or irritated. But, to his surprise, the master still smiled amiably at him, seemingly imperturbable and composed.

Mr. Su then asked the master, "Master, what about me? What do I look like?"

The master replied, "Oh, Mr. Su, you look like Buddha."

Mr. Su was surprised at his reponse. "Why do you say this?" he asked the master. "Why do you speak such nice words to me after I ridiculed you, saying that you look like a pile of ugly bullshit? Aren't you annoyed?"

The master smiled and said, "I see that you look like Buddha because my heart resides in him, or the Buddha is in me. For me, everything looks like Buddha. What you have in your heart is only bullshit. That's why you see others as bull-shit. If you set your mind on humanity," the master continued, "you will be free from evil thoughts. If you want to clean or change the nation, you must clean and change your heart first."

Feeling deeply ashamed, Mr. Su immediately bowed and thanked the master for his wise words.

Traditional story, Joseph Jiang, S.J., Manila, Philippines

Honesty on the Street

One Friday afternoon, my mother and I decided to catch up on some shopping at the Eastern Plaza. Stuck in a traffic jam, we saw a very sweet-looking girl selling flowers on the street. My mother called out to her to buy some flowers, more out of compassion for the girl than because of the beauty of the flowers. After paying for the flowers, my mother asked the driver to go on, forgetting that she had not received her change from the girl. As the vehicle started speeding off, the girl ran to keep up with the car, holding the change in her hand. When she caught up with us, my mother told her that she could keep the change. The girl, however, refused, explaining to my mother that she simply could not accept. We were quite astonished to see a little girl set such an example of honesty—which we often fail to do.

Adapted from a story by Mohammed Fahim Hara
in "Dhaka Diary," Star Weekend Magazine
Father Bob McCahill, M.M., Dhaka, Bangladesh

Moments of Reverence

In many secular Japanese hospitals, when a patient dies, the body is placed in a special room "where the spirit rests." For a few hours before the body is taken away, hospital personnel can go there to pay their respects to the family and to the person they had in their care. It is a reverent moment that means so much to all.

Sister Kathleen Reiley, M.M., Japan

Last Night I Had a Nightmare

Last night I had a very unusual dream, a nightmare really. I saw my entire state in anarchy. I witnessed shoot-outs, women and children being thrown into fires, and terror created among peace-loving people by plunderers who raped, killed, and tortured people to death. I was standing alone in the chaos, wondering how the peace-loving people of my country could be so inhuman toward other human beings.

Their hatred seemed to have no cause, but it had moved them to commit horrible crimes. Blood for blood had become the *modus operandi* and, within the blink of an eye, my peaceful land was sodden with blood. I was the only one alive and I was searching for my family. They were nowhere and I knew I had lost my world.

Sunrise came, but brought no meaning. Having lost everything, I had no reason to live. Then I saw a young, innocent child playing in blood that had been spilled on the street. He had no clue that, like me, he had lost his paradise. I couldn't resist picking him up and placing a tender kiss on his forehead. I promised myself that I would live for this child and try to give him a world where he could experience peace and tranquility. Then I kissed him once again, and he smiled his innocent smile.

Dream recounted by Alankar Khanal
to Father Joe Thaler, M.M., Nepal

The Importance of Family

"In the time of test, family is best."
Burmese proverb

Although many sweeping changes are impacting life in Asia, the centrality of marriage and the family remains deeply anchored in Asian societies. Nuclear families are close-knit, and the extended family provides a deep sense of belonging and identity. The majority of families in Asia are rural and, like rural people everywhere, they share a natural closeness to God's creation.

Both children and the elderly have a special place within the Asian family. Children are cherished and treasured as gifts of God, and parents willingly undertake various sacrifices to provide for their health, education, and well-being. And the elderly, parents and grandparents, have a revered position within family structures. Their advice is continually sought and they are loved and honored. In addition, in most Asian societies people have a strong reverence for their departed ancestors. The social values of filial piety and family loyalty are very important throughout Asia.

However, Asian families do not exist in cultural isolation. Today they are subject to and even threatened by an array of forces, including marital breakups, poverty, secularization, and consumerism. Although such social factors impact the very structures of marriage and family cohesion, it is not an overstatement to assert that the Asian family remains an abundant reservoir from which all members drink and are refreshed.

How to Discipline a Naughty Boy

One time I asked a Chinese priest friend, "When you were young and were naughty, how did your mother punish you? Did she scold you?"

He answered, "My mother would never scold me. No, she would sit me down and she would say, 'You are Chinese. Chinese people don't act this way.' I would feel so ashamed that I would cry."

Throughout the world, Chinese people are noted for their respect for their ancestors. Chinese people never want to shame their ancestors. These ancestors have given their descendants not only life but also an example of "how to be a real man" or "how to be a real woman." By their example, the ancestors teach, encourage, and inspire the succeeding generations.

Father Eugene F. Thalman, M.M., Hong Kong

Filial Love—Two Stories

Tang Sun, a disciple of Confucius, lived during the Zhou dynasty. Early in life he lost his mother. His father subsequently married another woman, who bore him two more children. She disliked and maltreated Tang. In winter she clothed him in garments made of rushes, while her own children wore cotton and fur clothes. Tang drove his father's cart to earn money to support the family, but eventually he became ill. Tang carefully concealed all his sufferings and refused to indulge in any complaint, even while enduring severe cold and hunger.

When his father finally learned the whole story, he determined to divorce his second wife. But Tang said, "No, please don't do this, Father. While Mother remains, only one son is cold, but if she departs, then three sons will suffer, and Mother will suffer also." The father then changed his mind, and after this the mother was led to repentance and became a good parent.

The filial piety of Tang moved Heaven to direct a female spirit in human form to go and help him. Eventually their family became rich, while Tang and his other two stepbrothers still maintained their filial love for their parents.

During the Ming dynasty there lived a young man named Huang Liang. He was from a peasant family in a rural area and he had parents who were getting old and sick. He served them with total love and obedience. In summer, when it was hot, he fanned and cooled their pillows and bed, and in winter, when it was cold, he warmed the bed for them with his body. When his parents wanted to taste fish in winter, but he didn't have enough money to buy fish, he would go to the frozen river and lay his body on it to defrost a hole to catch fish. When the heat of summer made it difficult to sleep, Huang would take a fan and slowly wave it so his parents could sleep soundly.

Having learned of Huang's piety, the emperor sent him an honorary banner as a mark of distinction and invited Huang to serve in the court. Huang refused, responding to the emperor with a message that said, "Your Majesty, although I should desire to serve in the court, I cannot leave my parents behind while they need my care and love. I must choose my parents over the court. For my parents' sake, I must live with poverty rather than wealth and honor."

The emperor was pleased with Huang's response and sent him two hundred pieces of silver to care for his parents.

Traditional stories, Joseph Jiang, S.J., Manila, Philippines

A Vietnamese Proverb

Ta vet a tam ao ta;
du trong du duc,
ao nha cung hon.

Come back and bathe in your own pond;
Clear or muddy, the home pond is always better.

Peter Phan, Mission and Catechesis:
Alexandre de Rhodes & Inculturation
in Seventeenth-Century Vietnam
(Orbis Books, 1998)

The End of the Cow

Upon his death, a father bequeathed the family cow to his two sons. The clever older son gave his younger brother the front end of the cow and took the back half for himself. The result was that the younger brother had to feed his end of the cow, while the older brother got all the milk.

The older brother made all the decisions pertaining to selling the milk and sharing the profits. The younger brother felt marginalized because he didn't participate in the decisions that affected his life. His family was always hungry, while his brother lived in luxury. This was certainly not what his father had intended. After a long time, the younger brother became very frustrated. He shot his end of the cow and the other end died too.

Parable adapted from Thou Shalt Think and Do:
Adventures with the Social Teachings of the Catholic Church
(*Asian Center for the Progress of Peoples, 2004*)

A Simple Witness

In the Philippines, the state views overseas Filipino workers (OFWs) as the country's new heroes because of their contributions to the economy. They leave their families behind, risk many dangers, and battle loneliness in foreign lands to provide a better life for their families back home.

Women make up many of the hundreds of thousands of OFWs who leave every year. Many of these women migrants work abroad as domestic workers, performing work that frees their employers from the tedious details of everyday life—cleaning, cooking, washing, ironing, minding children, and taking care of the sick or elderly. Because domestic work is not covered by labor laws, many women migrants are vulnerable to abuse and exploitation. Not surprisingly, many women migrants pray for a "good" employer.

Long working hours, inadequate food, and delayed or non-payment of wages are among the common problems domestic workers face. In addition, the work entails other hazards that inflict private pain. One migrant said that her employer did not even call her by name but instead addressed her as "slave-girl."

Clara was in her early twenties when she decided to work in Singapore. As the eldest in her family, she wanted to help her parents support her younger siblings. Although she had a degree in education, she could not find a job as a teacher in the Philippines or elsewhere. She prayed for a good employer in Singapore who would not hinder her faith life. Her prayers were answered, as her employer gave her days off on Sundays to attend Mass.

Clara found the work demanding. In addition to doing the household chores, she was entrusted with the household budget and helped the children with their schoolwork. The parents were out most of the time, so, for all practical purposes, Clara was the children's mother. When her employers' marriage broke up, she felt responsible for the children, whom she considered family. She had thought of working in Hong Kong where salaries are higher, but because her employer and the children had become her family, she stayed on.

The care and concern Clara showed to her family in the Philippines and her "family" in Singapore speak eloquently of the value of everyday acts of kindness and service.

Maruja M. B. Asis, Scalabrini Migration Center,
Manila, Philippines

A Father's Emotions

After receiving news that I would graduate with a B.A. with "Honors," I was on my way home in a rickshaw, when I saw an old teacher of mine crossing the road. Immediately I stopped my rickshaw and got down to speak to him and let him know my examination results. He was clearly happy for me. I invited him home and got back on my rickshaw. The rickshaw *walla* [rickshaw puller] then asked me about my results and even congratulated me. I was on the top of the world!

After reaching home, I brought out my wallet to pay for the ride. The rickshaw *walla* refused to take the fare.

"*Baba*," he said. "I am very happy for you today. My son took the same exams, but he failed. You are just like my son and I couldn't take money from you today." Saying this, he rushed away. His emotions touched me deep inside and somehow made my day even better than before.

Adapted from a story by Madmudul Hassan in "Dhaka Diary,"
Star Weekend Magazine
Father Bob McCahill, M.M., Dhaka, Bangladesh

The Tears of Lady Meng

This happened in the reign of the wicked, unjust Emperor Ch'in Shih Huang-ti. He was afraid that the Huns would break into the country from the north and not leave him any peace. In order to keep them in check, he decided to build a wall along the whole northern frontier of China. But no sooner was one piece built than another fell down, and the wall made no progress.

Then a wise man said to him: "A wall like this, which is over ten thousand miles long, can be built only if you immure a human being in every mile of the wall. Each mile will then have its guardian."

It was easy for the emperor to follow this advice, for he regarded his subjects as so much grass and weeds, and the whole land began to tremble under this threat. Plans were then made for human sacrifice in great numbers.

At the last minute, "an ingenious scholar" suggested to the emperor that it would be sufficient to sacrifice a man called Wan "since 'Wan' means ten thousand." Soldiers were dispatched at once to seize Wan, who was sitting with his bride at the wedding feast. He was carried off by the heartless soldiers, leaving Lady Meng, his bride, in tears.

Eventually, heedless of the fatigues of the journey, she traveled over mountains and through rivers to find the bones of her husband. When she saw the stupendous wall, she did not know how to find the bones. There was nothing to be done, and she sat down and wept. Her tears so affected the wall that it collapsed and laid bare her husband's bones.

When the emperor heard of Meng Chiang and the lengths to which she had gone to find her husband's bones, he wanted to see her himself. So, he sent for her, and she was brought before him. Her unearthly beauty so struck him that he decided to make her his empress. She knew she could not avoid her

fate, and therefore she agreed, but only on three conditions. First, a festival lasting forty-nine days was to be held in honor of her husband; second, the emperor, with all his officials, would be present at the burial; and third, he was to build a terrace forty-nine feet high on the bank of the river, where she wanted to make a sacrifice to her husband. Ch'in Shih Huang-ti granted all her requests at once.

When everything was ready, she climbed onto the terrace and began to curse the emperor in a loud voice for all his cruelty and wickedness. Although this made the emperor very angry, he held his peace. But when she jumped from the terrace into the river, he flew into a rage and ordered his soldiers to cut up her body into little pieces and grind her bones to powder.

When they did this, the little pieces changed into little silver fish, in which the soul of faithful Meng Chiang lives forever.

Traditional story told by C. S. Song
The Tears of Lady Meng (*Orbis Books, 1982*)

Children Are Cherished

Holimon, a typical Bengali Muslim woman, has attractive features, a brown complexion, and a gold ornament in her nose. Her body is wrapped in a solid-colored sari that covers her head, and she carries on her hip the youngest of her four children. No posture better explains her life and work than her embrace of Shah Alom, fourteen months of age. Childbearing and childrearing give Holimon status in the community, because everyone respects a mother.

A mother who must run an errand outside the compound in which her family lives will always take along her child. The child protects his mother's reputation whenever she enters into public view. The child is a sign that she is no frivolous person. A village woman who has no child wants to enjoy the respect that children-in-arms afford to their mothers. Thus, when necessity moves her into the marketplace or any other public place, the childless woman may borrow a neighbor's child. The Bengali Muslim village woman has the assurance of safe passage and honorable treatment because of the child in her arms.

True story, Father Bob McCahill, M.M., Bangladesh

Caring for One Another
in Community

"The most precious gift we can offer others is our presence."
Thich Nhat Hanh

The desire for community is a fundamental human longing. Instinctively, people sense that it is only through being with others that we can achieve authentic humanity. This thirst for an experience of communion is deep within every Asian's heart.

Nowhere does community emerge spontaneously or automatically, without dedicated effort. Solidarity and unity are not easily attained. They cannot be captured, preserved in a bottle, and then opened and served at will.

The experience of Asian peoples illustrates that community grows in the soil of sharing and caring. Generosity, sharing, and hospitality (so very Asian!) are often found among persons of meager resources. Generosity begets generosity, and its children are communion and solidarity. As fire exists by burning, community exists by daily sharing and caring.

Given Asia's diversity of religions and traditions, experiences of community (beyond the family) for most Asians will often involve people from other traditions. Buddhists, Muslims, Hindus, and Christians, all persons of good will work together to help each other. In a word, their focus is guided by "good neighbor-ology"—the daily living together in harmony and peace.

Sharing in the Philippines

Anywhere in the Philippines, if your neighbor borrows your soup tureen or serving platter, it will never return empty. Your neighbors will have cooked something for you.

In rural areas, everything is communal. The missing ingredients of a vegetable dish come from other backyards. You can plan meals around Susing's squash leaves, Oyong's green papayas, and the string beans in Naty's patch. Of course, the chili for the whole neighborhood comes from your own bush.

To Filipinos, the sense of sharing is also a way of maximizing every resource to the fullest. Rivers, trees, wells, farm animals, irrigation systems, fishing boats, and TV sets are shared.

Filipinos never forget to share good fortune either. A native sweets manufacturer someone helped while he was still struggling will not forget to send a gift basket every Christmas, for years on end, considerably more than would be required to repay a kindness. This is why a homecoming Filipino is easy to spot in an airport—he is so overloaded: lotions, soaps, and chocolates in one overnight bag, t-shirts, make-up, fancy jewelry, and fruits in another. A *pasalubong* or homecoming present for everyone is a Filipino institution.

Sharing is such a part of the Filipino psyche that it permeates the language. The word for brother or sister is *kapatol* or *kapatid*, a piece of your umbilical cord; a spouse is *kabiyak ng puso*, half of your heart; a close friend is *kabagang*, one of your teeth.

Father James H. Kroeger, M.M., Maryknoll Language School,
Davao City, Philippines

The Right Spirit of Youth

In one of the big public high schools here in Phnom Penh, some students in the graduating class understand the spirit of compassion.

A classmate, Eng Neang, lost his bicycle to a thief. Neang is from a poor family that doesn't have the money to buy him a new bike. How will he get from home to school and back again? There is no public transport and the motorcycle taxis are too expensive for poor Cambodians.

However, members of the class, on their own, took up a collection and have bought Neang a new bicycle so that he can finish high school with his classmates.

Youth are the hope of the future. With young people like this, a bright future lies ahead for Cambodia.

True story, Father James P. Noonan, M.M., Phnom Penh, Cambodia

Performing Children

Putul (her name means "doll") cannot yet walk. The ten-month-old girl can, however, stand up straight if someone helps her. Thus, Golenor can be seen playing with her wee neighbor, holding her upright while the shaky little girl tries to please her. Golenor smiles her encouragement to Putul and Putul is glad to win the smile.

This is how villagers entertain themselves. The children perform, the adults appreciate. Nowhere in rural Bangladesh are there toy stores—nor is there any need for them. The children make their own toys and design their own games. Relatives and friends encourage children to recite poetry or sing songs while standing in formal poses. The children's feet are planted on the bare earth, but it is as if they were on a stage, basking in the admiring gaze of their elders. Children grow up realizing that they have the ability to please others. Every child is an entertainer and knows that she or he has the ability to give joy to others.

Father Bob McCahill, M.M., Dhaka, Bangladesh

Hospitality in the Marshall Islands

Hency, an eight-year-old in our mission school on Arno Atoll, was striding along the beach, swinging a vine strung with his catch of nine fish. When he met my colleague, Janet, he stopped to exchange the traditional handshake and *yokwe* greeting. Then he slid two fish off his line. "One for you, Sister Janet, and one for Sister Joan," he said with a smile. Janet protested, knowing that the boy's father was off the island and that those fish had to feed eleven mouths. But the joy in Hency's eyes overcame all resistance. Off he went, shoulders back, head high, one in spirit with the traditional hospitality of the people of the Marshall Islands.

True story, Sister Joan Crevcoure, M.M., Marshall Islands

The Present Moment

When you open your eyes,
You open your mind;
When you open your mind,
You open your heart;
When you open your heart,
You live with dignity;
When you live with dignity,
You share divine life;
When you share divine life,
You can build a community of love;
When you build a community of love,
You enter eternity;
When you enter eternity,
Nothing can harm you;
When nothing can harm you,
You will live forever,
Even now in this present moment.

English translation by Joseph Petulla
The Tao Te Ching and the Christian Way
(Orbis Books, 1998)

The Case of the Generous Traveler

Chinese people are noted for their generosity. Some forty years ago, there was much poverty in China. People from Hong Kong visiting relatives on the mainland would always bring them bundles of clothing and food.

I will always remember one account from the newspaper. It seems that a merchant went to the mainland to visit relatives. He packed many gifts. When he returned to Hong Kong, he was wearing a pair of shorts and rubber shoes. That was all! The man explained that, at the end of his visit, having seen the poverty of his relatives, he gave them the clothes he had in his suitcase, the suitcase itself, and then most of the clothes he was wearing. The Hong Kong newspaper pointed out that this kind of behavior was not unusual—visitors often returned from the mainland similarly attired.

Father Eugene F. Thalman, M.M., Hong Kong

Samnang

Samnang, a deaf woman in her early twenties, appeared one day at the door of our project for the deaf. Apparently she knew no sign language. She could not read or write, and she had only the clothes she was wearing. How she found us is a mystery. Slowly, using gestures and drawing pictures, we learned she had no family and was homeless.

We were teaching sign language and basic literacy to deaf people too old to have attended the first school for the deaf started in 1997. Although we had already planned to start a hostel for homeless deaf people, Samnang's arrival forced us to move up our plans. We found her a place to stay and enrolled her in our beginner's class.

She progressed well and became more independent and self-assured. When it was time to stop classes for a period of teacher training, we asked Samnang to serve as a volunteer in a project that cares for babies with AIDS. It was there that Samnang found her calling.

The staff there didn't know sign language, but they and Samnang soon learned to communicate. The director noticed her engaging smile and her gentleness with the babies and after a few weeks offered her a job as a caregiver. She was delighted and so were we.

On the day when she was to move from our hostel to the group home for the babies, she was going to hire a cyclo (a three-wheeled pedal-powered vehicle used to haul people and goods) but found she had no money. I lent her four dollars, cautioning her that she had to pay me back when she got her first paycheck and also that she should start saving money from her salary. She had a job, but her future was far from secure.

Two weeks later, when I saw Samnang at a gathering for the deaf, she came over to report excitedly that her new job was going well. Then she pulled out a ten-dollar bill and started to put it in my pocket. I told her she owed me only four dollars, but she said that since I was old (I'm in my early sixties) and single (I'm a priest) and without anyone to care for me, I needed to put the money aside for my old age. It was only with difficulty that I assured her that I would be well taken care of in the future and that she should keep the six dollars for her own future well-being. Hers will certainly be more difficult than mine.

True story, Father Charles Dittmeier, Phnom Penh, Cambodia

Hospitality

When I was traveling from Dhaka to a small village in Bangladesh, our bus broke down. As I started walking, I made friends with some of the other passengers. When we arrived in another little village, a Muslim family offered me hospitality in their small straw house. It was getting dark and there would be no transportation until the next morning, so I accepted their offer. The couple gave me their bed while the children slept on the floor.

I was kept awake most of the night by the Muslim couple who stayed up all night singing and talking by a fire outside the little house. I could not figure out what was going on. The following day I asked why they had stayed up all night. I was told that they wanted to make sure that I, a foreign stranger, would not be harmed by any of their enemies, since I was probably carrying valuables. Their generosity of spirit and action touched me deeply.

Father Richard T. Ouellette, M.M., Bangladesh

The Conversion of a Thief

In the late 1980s in Shanghai, a notorious, cunning man named Lee San lived by thieving. He was a superb and highly skilled thief who had never been caught and boasted that he could steal whatever he wanted.

One day he was wandering in the street, searching for a target. Wang Wu, a friend, called out to him: "Lee, guess what? I have great news. A certain family has just received a few thousand dollars. They are an old couple and I know where their house is."

"Aha!" Lee San laughed. "I'll take this on tonight."

"But they have a big and ferocious wolf dog, so you may have a problem."

Lee San replied, "So what? It's just a stupid dog. Don't underestimate my skill!"

It was a pitch-dark night, and the wind was howling. Lee San took his tools and headed straight for the street where the old couple lived. When he arrived, he saw a big lantern hung high at the gate of the house. He began moving in, softly and quietly, when suddenly, a dog began barking. Lee San saw a huge dog behind the gate and quickly threw it a piece of poisonous meat. A few seconds later the dog fell to the ground. Lee San stealthily opened the gate. He went up to the door, opened it, and made his way quickly to the bedroom where he found the money under a pillow. "This was so easy," Lee San thought. "They have so much money yet they don't have a vault to secure it. Are they stingy?"

Then he heard voices in the next room. The old woman and her husband were talking. Lee stayed where he was and listened carefully to make sure they hadn't heard him.

"Old fellow, should we spend some money to hire a maid to take care of us? Both of us are blind and old, so how will we survive as the time passes?" It was the weary voice of an old woman.

Lee San was surprised. If they were blind, why had they put up a big lantern in front of their gate?

"Oh, yes, my dear, you are right. But where can we find the money to hire a maid?" replied an old man.

"Didn't we just get a few thousand dollars for the loss of our son in that accident? Why don't we use that money?"

"Are you crazy, wife? Don't you remember that we decided to donate that money to build an orphanage? Did you forget?"

Listening, Lee San grew uneasy.

"Oh, oh, yes. See how bad my memory is! I had forgotten. I'm getting old and useless. Still, we could save money by not buying oil for the lamp, and we could sell our dog Ding Ding."

"But we must light the way for people on the street. The street has no light and people who travel in the evening can't see their way in the dark. And if Ding Ding is here, then people no longer have to fear bandits or thieves when they come down the street."

"You're right," said the old woman, "It's too bad we didn't have another son when we were still young." The old woman

sighed. "But never mind. Let's get back to work. We still have stacks of paper boxes to be pasted together."

Lee San sneaked quietly outside. Then, sitting down in front of the gate, he began to sob. He himself was an orphan who had been adopted and later escaped from his violent step-father and uncaring family.

The following morning, two things were left at the door of the old couple's house—the money and an exquisite vault.

After that, no one ever saw Lee San again. He disappeared like a small cloud. Someone said that he entered a monastery and others that he became a Buddhist. Still others said that he became a philanthropist. In any case, a few years later, several orphanages and homes for the elderly were built in the name of Lee San.

Joseph Jiang, S.J., Manila, Philippines

Little Vince

What's in a name? Well, if you're a member of the Asmat tribe, quite a lot. A name encompasses a person's life spirit and source of being. Giving a person your name or having a person named after you presumes a sharing in the same life source or spirit, a sharing of strength as well as an indivisible common identity. This is a concept not easily grasped by an overly rational mind.

When I arrived in Irian-Jaya, I was already aware of this, but it wasn't until my catechist named his son after me that I became personally aware of the deeply spiritual role a name plays in these people's lives.

One day the catechist's wife came over to wash the dishes. As usual, little Vince tagged along. I had just settled down for a short siesta and little Vince was making quite a fuss. His mother tried valiantly to quiet him down but without much success. Finally, I heard her say in an exasperated voice, "Be quiet, Vince, you are sleeping."

That simple sentence spoke volumes. Everything seemed to gel for me in that instant. Since then, an enhanced awareness of my spirit/God connection with little Vince has changed my whole outlook on our relationship, mutual connectedness, and responsibility to one another.

Around here, if someone is named after you, it's no longer "Hi, how are you?" but rather "Hi, how am I?" Or "Hey, where am I going?" or "What am I going to do today?"

Confusing? Just stop and think about it for a while. It actually makes perfect sense.

True story, Father Vince Cole, M.M., Papua, Indonesia

Receiving Gifts

I get much satisfaction from helping others, especially here in Hong Kong. However, I am not comfortable receiving help from others. Still, the kindest thing I can do for others is to let them do something for me. People bring me fruit, cookies, and awful tasting medicine for my ailments. Sometimes they give me a red packet and say, "Buy something to eat." These gifts come from people who are certainly much poorer than I am. But it would be devastating to tell someone, "You are too poor to give me a gift." I need to let people love me and then later figure out how to redistribute the gifts they have given me.

Father Eugene F. Thalman, M.M., Hong Kong

A Traditional Healer, Priests, and a Psychologist

In a remote village of East Timor lives an old woman known as a *matan-do 'ok* (someone who reads the present in light of the past and the future). Although her hut is old and small, she welcomes everyone who comes for healing. She asks the same three questions of each person.

The first question she asks is, how do you feel about yourself? She asks this question because she is convinced that how one feels about one's self contributes to one's health.

Her second question is, how do you feel about your neighbors? She holds that a person can get sick when a relationship with a neighbor is broken, because brokenness causes emotional instability.

Her third question is, how do you relate with other creatures? Do you respect all creatures? Her fundamental belief is that whatever one experiences, whether good health or sickness, is brought about by how one lives one's life.

After listening attentively to the stories of her patients, the *matan-do 'ok* usually asks them to honestly examine their lives to see if there is any brokenness or distortion. When a patient recognizes that an illness has been caused by hatred, be it toward self, neighbor, or anything else, then the *matan-do 'ok* will encourage that person to begin a dialogue with himself or herself, with another person, or with nature. Restored relationships are essential for real healing.

One time some priests went to visit the *matan-do 'ok*. They told her to stop her "pagan" healing practice. Then a well-trained psychologist went to analyze the *matan-do 'ok* and concluded that her healing practice was that of an uneducated and uncivilized person who did not understand how to heal emotional hurts.

After the priests and the psychologist had silenced and dismissed the *matan-do 'ok*, the priests preached about dialogue, reconciliation, and peace with one's self, one's neighbor, all other creatures, and God, while the psychologist spread the civilized and educated message about getting in touch with one's own inner feelings toward self and others.

Clemente Moreira, FdCC, Lospalos, East Timor

Basketball

As a young American and seminarian, I really enjoyed playing basketball. It was my favorite sport. In the seminary we played almost every day. Once on the court, we humble seminarians became bloodthirsty demons. Theologically, we agreed that winning wasn't everything, but in the heat of a game you could never convince any of us that it was "only a game."

I was in for a shock when I arrived at my first assignment in Hong Kong. A group of young Chinese men playing basketball on our school playground invited me to join in. I thought I would teach them how the game should be played. Instead, they taught me.

According to an American custom, when an opponent is taking a shot, you wave your hand right in front of his face like an airplane propeller. Instead, these lads folded their arms and watched the opponent take an undistracted shot. It didn't seem very competitive to me.

Next, five or six little children decided to play right in the middle of the court. My immediate reaction was to tell them to go elsewhere, thinking that if they didn't move, we would take stronger measures for the "children's own good." To my great surprise, the young Chinese men didn't say a word to the children. They just played a wide path around them.

Today, things have changed as young people imitate the competitive spirit and techniques of Western sports stars. Yet, as I walk through the park, I frequently see signs of traditional gentleness among our Chinese youth. When playing games, there is no need to set boundaries or keep score. It is fun just to play.

True story, Maryknoll missioner, Hong Kong

Caring Is a Weapon

Everyone says that my way of life is the way
    of a simpleton.
Being largely the way of a simpleton is what
    makes it worthwhile.
If it were not the way of a simpleton
It would long ago have been worthless.
These possessions of a simpleton being the
    three I choose and cherish:
To care,
To be fair,
To be humble.
When a man cares he is unafraid,
When he is fair he leaves enough for others,
When he is humble he can grow;
Whereas if, like men of today,
He be bold without caring,
Self-indulgent without sharing,
Self-important without shame,
He is dead.
The invincible shield of caring
Is a weapon from the sky against being dead.

Excerpt from The Way of Life, according to Lao Tzu
    (New York: John Day Company, 1944)

Culture Matters

"Ten people, ten colors."
Japanese proverb

Asia encompasses a rich diversity of cultures, each defined by its own values, rituals, music, language, poetry, art, and wisdom. Each culture is, in fact, a unique way of being human that emerges from the life and activity of human groups. In turn, persons within a group are shaped by that culture.

In the cultures of Asia, we meet the beauty of Asia's peoples. Their cultural heritages reveal precious elements of truth, holiness, goodness, and creativity. Culture can include everything from the very mundane to the practice of fine art: from negotiating a traffic circle in Phnom Penh, Cambodia, to the intricacies of Japanese haiku or Chinese calligraphy.

Readers may notice that several of the stories in this section have been contributed by expatriate missioners with long experience in Asia. A simple logic underlies this fact. These long-term residents have come to deeper insights into life and faith from the interaction of their two cultures—their birth culture and their adopted culture. In a sense, they have become "doubly human," a gift that is a great treasure.

Readers may smile at some stories in this section and wonder at others. In any case, think of this small sampling as an invitation to learn more about the many cultures present in Asia today.

Feeding the Hungry Ghosts

The Chinese people, who have a loyal devotion to those who have died, take obligations to their deceased relatives and ancestors very seriously.

Tio Bi Le, a factory worker, was the first catechumen in Shalu parish in Taiwan. When she neared the end of her study of doctrine, I said to her, "You are the first one in your family and your village to become Catholic. What do your parents think about it?"

She answered, "My father isn't opposed but my mother says I will become a hungry ghost after I die because no one will put out food for me. But I told my mother, 'Don't worry. I listened to the Catholic teaching very carefully, and for Christians there is an everlasting banquet after death. I won't be a hungry ghost.'"

True story, Father Eugene M. Murray, M.M.,
Taichung Hsien, Taiwan

Pigs—No Pigs

The Asmat people are pragmatic, and their pragmatism includes their relationship with the spirit world. Spirits, in myriad shapes, sizes, and classes, play a central role in their lives and determine to a large extent what they do at any given time. Maybe it is this intimate familiarity with the spirits that allows for a certain degree of pragmatism to permeate their relationship.

Once I was far upriver attending a male initiation feast in the village of Mumugu. This sacred event, intricate and laden with rich symbolism, can last for months. Naturally, the spirits play a major role in its unfolding.

At a particular point in the feast I attended, the hunters needed an answer from the spirits to the question of whether they would have a successful pig hunt. They fashioned a flat oblong piece of wood about eight inches long and attached a cord to it through a hole in one end. After painting the object with clay and clamshell powder, the men huddled intensely around the main fireplace. "What's going on?" I whispered to my friend Menja over the sound of the drums.

"We are consulting with the spirits. The spirits' voice speaks through that wooden object. The spirits will say either 'pigs' or 'no pigs.' If the spirits say 'pigs' then our hunt will be successful."

Just then, the drumming stopped and one of the men began violently whirling the "spirit voice" over his head. It soon began emanating weird roaring sounds in a volume that rose and fell.

"What are the spirits saying?" I asked Menja.

"No pigs," he replied.

"Oh, bad luck," I said. "Does that mean there will be no pig meat for the feast?"

Menja just smiled at me as he reached for the "spirit voice" and began refashioning it with his machete.

This is not so very unlike the relationship of Christians with the spirit world, really. I remember my mother dressing the Infant of Prague in pink clothes with the promise that they would immediately be changed to blue if I passed my exams.

True story, Father Vince Cole, M.M., Papua, Indonesia

Jade

For more than twenty-four hundred years, the Chinese have admired jade and used it as a treasured gift. Jade, which is hard and dense, is wonderful to touch. It also has subtle optical proprieties and makes a lovely sound when struck.

Confucius praised the virtues of jade. He said that superior men in ancient times discovered that jade symbolized the five virtues of kindness, wisdom, integrity, courage, and purity. In his *Book of Rites* Confucius described jade as soft, smooth, and glossy (when polished), like benevolence; fine, compact, and strong, like intelligence; angular, but not sharp and cutting, like righteousness; and (when struck) like music. Like loyalty, its flaws do not conceal its beauty, nor its beauty its flaws.

Who needs a meditation book when holding a precious piece of jade?

Description of the virtues of jade adapted from Li Chi, *attributed to Confucius*

The Stone of Jade

Over five hundred years before Christ, there was a man named Bian He. He found a large stone that was actually an unpolished piece of jade. Bian He presented it to the emperor. The emperor saw nothing but a large stone, thought he was being tricked, and ordered Bian He's left foot to be chopped off.

Bian He later sent the same present to the next emperor, who also saw only a stone and ordered Bian He's right foot to be chopped off.

When a third emperor came to the throne, Bian He stood outside the emperor's palace holding the stone in his arms and wept for three days and three nights. The emperor sent someone to investigate, then ordered the stone to be polished. Only then did they discover a beautiful piece of jade revealed.

From Han Feizi, *adapted from a quotation in Bishop John Tong,*
Challenges and Hopes: Stories from the Catholic Church in China
(Taipei: Wisdom Press, 1999)

Culture Clash

The Muyu tribe of Irian-Jaya are a people who are tenacious, thrifty, superstitious, and often strongly opinionated. A Catholic priest, a friend of mine, reflected on a dilemma he experienced in preaching to them. "Isn't it strange," he said, "that we come halfway across the world to preach about God to the Muyu tribe? We herd people of every sex and age into the church and proceed to reveal to them God's most sacred mysteries. We shout the words over the din of a noisy congregation, often using loudspeakers, in order to get this most sacred of messages across. The louder we can make it, the better it seems.

"What must these Muyu people think? It is a frontal attack on their way of dealing with the sacred. For the Muyu, the most sacred of mysteries must be transmitted via revered whispers directly from mouth to ear. The mysteries must be revealed in stages, starting with the elders and ending with the young people, but only when they are judged able to absorb the profundity of the material. Only the most innocuous of messages can be discussed openly before young and old, male and female alike. To do this with the sacred is considered disrespectful. It prompts one to doubt the veracity of the content."

The challenge remains. What is the best way to present the word of God and allow it to express itself so that it can be heard amidst the richness of so many diverse cultures without reducing any of that richness?

True story, Father Vince Cole, M.M., Papua, Indonesia

Happy

Calligraphy, the drawing of Chinese characters, is a highly treasured art form in Chinese tradition. Many of the works in Chinese art galleries depict Chinese characters, and artists spend years perfecting their skills. They begin by tracing the characters of the "greats" and only later do they develop their individual style. When a master calligrapher draws a Chinese character, he seeks not only to express the meaning of the word the character represents but also to convey something of the feeling evoked by an understanding of that meaning.

When I was in the United States, I often showed the Chinese character depicted on the facing page to students who ranged from third-graders through university students. Without telling them the meaning of the character, I asked them how the character made them feel. The students invariably replied, "nothing" or "squiggly lines" or "weird" or "funny."

When I asked the same question of Chinese children in kindergarten or first or second grades, there was always at least one child who replied, "happy!" Yes, this is the Chinese character for "good fortune" that Chinese people paste on their doors each Chinese New Year. And the feeling evoked is certainly "happy!"

True story, Father Eugene F. Thalman, M.M., Hong Kong

Speak Carefully

A royal court minister saw a farmer tilling his field with two cows, one yellow and one red. The minister asked the farmer which cow was stronger, but got no reply. The official asked again, but the farmer kept working in silence. The minister fumed and then shouted.

Finally, the farmer approached him and whispered, "Sir, I think the yellow cow is stronger. But I couldn't answer you aloud because the red cow would hear and be disappointed."

From Sang-Hun Choe and Christopher Torchi, eds.
How Koreans Talk (*Unhengnamu, 2002*)
Father Edward Whalen, M.M., Seoul, Korea

The Tea Ceremony

Christians and those of other religious traditions can learn much from the Japanese tea ceremony. I know of one Christian whose spirituality *is* the tea ceremony. She has a great reverence for Sen Rikyu, probably the most revered of all the masters of tea. Many of the expressions that encapsulate the "spirit" of tea were, according to tradition, formulated by him. If we study the spirit of the tea ceremony we can understand why this woman finds the "way of tea" a method of practicing her faith.

Some of the expressions used to convey the spirit of the tea ceremony include these:

和　*wa*

敬　*kei*

清　*sei*

寂　*jaku*

和 *(wa)*, the character for peace, can also mean circle and moral goodness. When a group of people are gathered in the teahouse, they should be at peace with one another. The circle symbolizes the unity of their hearts. Sen Rikyu limited the space in his teahouse to four and a half tatami mats, forcing participants to sit close together in order to promote intimacy.

敬 *(kei)* is the character for respect or honor. Respect must be extended to all people and all things. The formality of the tea ceremony—the etiquette that characterizes the interactions of those involved in the ritual and the care with which the implements are treated—is an external sign of an inner attitude of profound respect.

清 *(sei)* is purity of heart, and has been likened to the purity mentioned by Jesus in the Sermon on the Mount. "Blessed are the pure in heart, for they will see God" (Matthew 5:8). When I heard this interpretation, I gained a new insight into that beatitude. You could say that *sei* means the presence of the divine.

寂 *(jaku)* literally translated means lonely, but that hardly does justice to the meaning here. It is the emptiness that a person experiences on arriving at nirvana. It is what Moses experienced as he approached the burning bush.

Father Eugene F. Thalman, M.M., Hong Kong

Cambodian Traffic

When new members of our Maryknoll organization arrive in Cambodia, we encourage them not to even consider driving a motorcycle or car for at least six months. They must first gain a sense of the rules and the flow of traffic here. All of us who have learned to drive elsewhere have a very different understanding of what is the "right" way to drive.

Some differences are very practical. For example, in Cambodia traffic never stops. First of all, there are only twenty or thirty traffic lights in the entire country—all of them in the capital, Phnom Penh—and no functioning stop signs. Also, most of the vehicles are small motorbikes, and it is inconvenient to downshift them and bring them to a halt.

Other differences are more cultural. In the United States, driving is based on individual rights. I pull up to an intersection and stop until I have the right of way. You go and then I go.

But in Cambodia, everyone has the right of way. There is no need to stop. A driver just pulls into an intersection—without even looking to see if it is safe—and all the traffic moves to one side or the other to let the newcomer in.

This can be infuriating for Western drivers who are prone to shout: "He pulled out right in front of me! He didn't even look!" And that is true. The Cambodian driver doesn't look because he knows that the traffic will adjust for him. It's the same for pedestrians who just walk out into traffic expecting it to flow around them.

For Westerners this is cause for road rage, but for Cambodians, it's just a different logic and a different way of working together.

Observation, Father Charles Dittmeier, Phnom Penh, Cambodia

Fan K'uan: His Painting and Our Prayer

One of my favorite ways of beginning prayer is to gaze at a painting by someone such as Fan K'uan, an eleventh-century Chinese artist.

When we view traditional Western paintings, our eyes first look at the foreground, then move up to the horizon, and finally settle on a single focus point.

When we look at a painting by Fan K'uan, our eyes follow a flow of water in the foreground up the mountain and into the beyond. Instead of arriving at a focus point, we find ourselves in limitless space.

The painting pulls me up into God's mystery. Since the painting has no focal point, my eyes may drop to focus on some detail, such as the tiny, nearly insignificant people in the foreground. I ask with the psalmist, "What is man that you should be mindful of him, or the son of man that you should care for him?" (Psalm 8:5).

I see the scraggly bushes clinging to the barren, steep mountainsides. Against tremendous odds, the little bushes are hanging on for dear life. I think of the poor of the world who cling to the life given them by God.

The traditional Chinese painting gives no indication of the time of day. It is a "now" experience. At any moment, our gaze may drift from some detail and again be gently swept up to the mountain heights and beyond into eternity, where for a brief period we can disappear into the mystery of God.

Meditation by an anonymous missioner

Chinese Readers Know Who Did It

In a Western detective story, the reader discovers "who did it" at the conclusion.

Not so with many traditional Chinese detective stories! In the very first pages, the author identifies the murderer.

The Chinese "detective" is not a detective but rather the judge in the case. While he has a couple of assistants to help him, he alone is responsible for establishing the guilt of the offender. He doesn't have a police department to do his leg work or forensics. The judge must not only discover the identity of the criminal but he must also get the culprit to admit his guilt. Only then will the judge impose the punishment.

The traditional judge may legally use torture to encourage a confession. However, the judge must be careful in employing torture. If he is mistaken, he himself will undergo similar torture.

Even worse, if the Chinese judge were to impose the death penalty and later discover his error, he would suffer the same fate.

The thrill for the reader lies in watching the judge catch the perpetrator.

Father Eugene F. Thalman, M.M., Hong Kong

Marriage Proposal

Cambodia has no social welfare system, so being old and alone can be terrible. An elderly person without family faces the possibilities of loneliness, deprivation, sickness, and even untimely death.

Although I don't think of myself as infirm and elderly (I'm a sixty-one-year-old priest in good health), the deaf people with whom I work are always concerned about my future, which, in their eyes, is rather bleak. They are continually telling me of their sister or their widowed aunt or a friend whom I should marry.

There are only five thousand Cambodian Catholics in the country, so there is little understanding of the Catholic Church or the role of a priest. In trying to explain the tradition of celibacy, I usually refer to the model of the Buddhist monks (Cambodia is 95 percent Buddhist) who do not marry so they can commit themselves more fully to their work. But that answer really doesn't satisfy those who worry about me.

Recently I was in southern Cambodia to help organize the deaf people there and offer them job training. One thirty-year-old deaf woman spoke about her wish to learn to sew and then switched the topic to marriage, saying that she would be married in three months. I listened attentively and said a silent prayer that she and her husband would have a successful marriage. She then gave me the phone number of her uncle and I said I would call him to let her know when the job training would start.

A week later she appeared at our office in Phnom Penh, agitated that I hadn't called her uncle. I was astonished by what I thought I understood from her signing, so I called Justin, our deaf English advisor, to help me understand more clearly. He confirmed what I thought I had understood. She was planning to marry *me* in three months!

Apparently she had been saying something similar three months before when I first met her, but because she had never mentioned marrying me, I had assumed she was speaking of marrying someone else. Apparently my attentiveness that day had been read as acceptance and now she was here to make the arrangements.

Justin and I sat with her for thirty minutes, gently explaining that as a priest I could not marry, but that I would still be her friend. Love is not a determining factor in marriages here, but I probably broke her heart. At thirty, she undoubtedly was experiencing the cultural pressure to marry, and a marriage between a deaf woman and a "rich" foreigner would have fulfilled her greatest dreams.

We parted friends, but I know that she was disappointed and probably very confused about why an "old" man would turn down such a good offer of someone to care for him in his old age.

True story, Father Charles Dittmeier, Phnom Penh, Cambodia

How Long-winded Can You Get?

Brevity and long-windedness are opposites—that is how opposed the values of the English and Pilipino languages are. Where English emphasizes brevity and getting directly to the point, Pilipino admires flowery and indirect expressions; where English teaches short speeches, Pilipino says the speeches must be long, since otherwise one would insult the audience. In fact, a very short speech is a sign of discourtesy and lack of regard for those who have come.

Here is an example: The speaker meant to say "Don't tempt me." But what he actually said was this: *"Kahoy na babad sa tubig, sa apoy huwag ilapit, pag nadagandang sa init, sapilitang magdirikit"* (Don't place a wet piece of wood near the fire as the heat will eventually cause it to burn).

Another example: The barrio captain gave his words of greeting and, in effect, said: *"Kung ako ay makapangyarihan lamang, kukunin kang lahat ang mga bituin sa langit, itutuhog sa tali at ilalagay sa inyong leeg. Aanihin ko ang ulap sa kaitaasan, hahabihin kong mistulang malasutlang dadaanan para sa mga yapak ninyo patungo sa aming kandungan"* (If I had but the power, I would gather all the stars in the heavens, entwine them into a garland and place it around your neck. I would harvest the clouds above, I would then weave them into a silken path for your footsteps toward our lap).

The English equivalent is just one word: "Welcome!"

Adapted from Juan M. Flavier's My Friends in the Barrios
(Quezon City: New Day Publishers, 1974)
Father James H. Kroeger, M.M., Manila, Philippines

Haiku

Haiku is a form of Japanese poetry that is always composed of three lines of seventeen syllables and written to reflect a person's feelings and thoughts. Haiku are noted for both their simplicity and their depth.

If I could bundle
Fuji's breezes back to town . . .
What a souvenir.
       Basho

I'm very sorry
To have to die at this time
With plum trees in bloom
       Raizan

The sea of all song
Is the farmer's busy hum
As he plants his rice.
       Basho

Linking the World through English II
(Philippines: Diwa Scholastic Press, 2006)

Wisdom from the Orient

"Never think of knowledge and wisdom as little."
Mongolian proverb

Wisdom literature can be found in all corners of the world, but Asia is especially known for its contemplative traditions and practices. Asia's great teachers of human wisdom and divine intuition include Lao Tzu, Confucius, Buddha, and, more recently, Gandhi. They speak of life's true values and its inner meaning, of reverence and respect and authentic human goodness. Proverbs, poetry, chants, and the sayings of sages or enlightened rulers are some of the literary forms that capture the "wisdom of the Orient."

The chief purpose of wisdom literature is to teach by providing practical norms for moral conduct, and the teaching is often done not by issuing commandments or juridical guidelines, but through the use of parables and proverbs so that all persons, not only the formally educated, can easily grasp the insights. Once understood, the insights are then translated into moral values, upright behavior, and deeds of service.

It is not surprising that the Hebrew scriptures, coming as they do from one of the lands of the Asian continent, abound with books of wisdom, such as Proverbs, and that Jesus is sometimes understood in Asia as a "wisdom guru" *par excellence*. Asia's holy books and inspired sages continue to illumine humanity's pilgrimage.

Knowledge

Disciple: What's the difference between knowledge and enlightenment?

Master: When you have knowledge, you use a torch to show the way. When you are enlightened, you become a torch.

William Dych, S.J., ed., Anthony de Mello
(Orbis Books, 1999)

Artistic Village

There was once a farming village in a remote area of northwest China. The village might have been named "Artistic Village."

Everyone from the youngest child to the oldest person was an artist. When the farming work was completed, the villagers went to their workshops. Some painted beautiful pictures, some carved large statues that almost seemed to be alive, and others wrote exciting epic poems. They had good farming land, so that they didn't have to sell any of their products. When they finished a work, they stored it in a large barn.

On the surface, it was a wonderful life. But something seemed to be missing, although no one could figure out what it was.

One day a traveler came to town and in the years that followed Artistic Village came to be known as Happy Artistic Village. The stranger supplied what was missing. What gift did the traveler bring?

When he wasn't farming, the stranger walked through the village, enjoying and praising the beautiful things that the villagers were making and all the beautiful things stored in the barn. Gradually, the villagers began to take some time off from their artistic work to walk around admiring and talking about the wonderful works of art that their fellow villagers were making. How their lives all changed!

God is a great artist. But we are often too busy doing stuff for God and our neighbor. We have no time to enjoy and praise God's artwork. Poor God. Poor artists! Poor all of us!

Parable, Father Eugene F. Thalman, M.M., Hong Kong

Zen and the Wolves

When wolves were discovered in the village near Master Shoju's Zen temple, he entered the graveyard nightly for all of one week and sat in meditation. Strangely enough, that put a stop to the wolves' prowling. Overjoyed, the villagers asked him to describe the secret rites he had performed.

"I didn't have to resort to such things," he said, "nor could I have done so. While I was in *zazen*, a number of wolves gathered around me, licking the tip of my nose, sniffing my windpipe. They did all sorts of silly things. But because I remained in the right state of mind, I wasn't bitten. As I keep preaching to you, the proper state of mind will make it possible for you to be free in life and death, invulnerable to fire and water. Even wolves are powerless against it. I simply tried to practice what I preach."

Adapted from
Zen: Poems, Prayers, Sermons, Anecdotes, Interviews
by Lucien Stryk and Takashi Ikemoto
(Doubleday, 1963)

Wisdom from Korea

Wisdom and humility go hand in hand. The ear of a rice stalk droops with weight as it ripens. The tree branch that bears the most fruit hangs lowest, just as a humble sage avoids the lime-light.

From Sang-Hun Choe and Christopher Torchi, eds.
How Koreans Talk *(Unhengnamu, 2002)*
Father Ed Whelan, M.M., Seoul, Korea

The Tribe and the Soldier

There is a small tribe in East Timor whose members believe that there are spirits in everything—stones, mountains, rivers, and trees. The people have a very strong conviction that trees, especially those growing on the mountains, have spirits that dwell within and among them. The tribe has ancient rules governing how trees are to be treated, and the members of the tribe have always been careful to obey the regulations handed down by their ancestors.

The first rule is that the trees must not be cut at will but only if needed to build houses for the tribe. Another rule is that the members must ask permission from the spirit dwelling in a tree before cutting it down so that the spirit will not be angry. If the spirit is angry, it will send water to destroy those living near the trees. The tribe had always followed these rules and no calamity had ever happened.

One day, a soldier came to the village to teach the tribe members to read and write. He soon gained a reputation as a learned man and was well respected. Although the soldier accepted some of the people's traditional beliefs and practices, he was arrogant and refused to follow others, including the belief that the trees had spirits and could not be cut down without having first obtained the spirits' permission. Because the soldier was very influential, he convinced some of the young people to cut down the big trees without following the traditional rites.

The elders protested that the traditional rites had to be followed to spare them from the wrath of the spirits of the trees. However, the soldier did not heed their protest. He had the trees cut down so that a school could be built. His plan was to educate the people, to teach them modern ways so that they would no longer believe in the spirits.

The elders were unable to intervene because the soldier had weapons and his strong young supporters threatened the elders. So, the soldier and his men cut down all the trees. Then they began building the school to educate and civilize the members of the tribe.

Unfortunately, just when they were about to finish the school, the rainy season came and the ensuing floods destroyed the whole village.

Clemente Moreira, FdCC, Lospalos, East Timor

The Thief Who Became a Disciple

One evening, as Shichiri Kojun was reciting sutras, a thief with a sharp sword entered, demanding either his money or his life.

Shichiri told him: "Do not disturb me. You can find the money in that drawer." Then he resumed his recitation.

A little while later he stopped and called, "Don't take it all. I need some to pay taxes tomorrow."

The intruder gathered up most of the money and started to leave. "Thank a person when you receive a gift," Shichiri added. The man thanked him and made off.

A few days later, the fellow was caught and confessed, among other things, his offense against Shichiri. When Shichiri was called as a witness he said: "This man is not thief, at least as far as I am concerned. I gave him the money and he thanked me for it."

After he had finished his prison term, the man went to Shichiri and became his disciple.

Adapted from a traditional Zen story

The Virtue of Patience

Once upon a time, there was a little boy who was very naughty and lazy about learning. His parents were very sad about this. One day, when he was playing along a canal, he saw an old woman holding an iron rod and sharpening it against a large rock. He approached the woman, but she did not notice him. He was so surprised at what the woman was doing that he asked, "Hello! What are you doing?"

Without looking up as she continued sharpening the iron rod, the woman replied, "You know, little boy, I want to make a needle out of this iron rod."

The little boy was even more surprised and asked the woman, "The iron rod is so big. How can you make a needle out of it?"

"If today I cannot make a needle, then I continue sharpening it tomorrow. The iron rod is indeed so big, but the longer you sharpen it, the smaller it gets. In the end, it will become a needle," replied the old woman.

The boy discovered that whatever we do requires patience, and no matter how difficult the work is, if we have persistence, we will succeed in the end.

Anonymous from Vietnam,
adapted from a quotation in
Prayer without Borders: Celebrating Global Wisdom
(Baltimore: Catholic Relief Services, 2004)

Using What Is Not

Thirty spokes converge on a hub;
What is not there makes the wheel useful.
Clay is shaped to form a pot;
What is not there makes the pot useful.
Doors and windows are cut to shape a room;
What is not there makes the room useful.
Take advantage of what is there
By making use of what is not.

Chapter 11, Tao te Ching *of Lao Tzu*

The Tunnel

Zenkai, the son of a samurai, journeyed to Edo and there became the retainer of a high official. He fell in love with the official's wife and was discovered. In self-defense, he slew the official and then ran away with the wife.

Both of them later became thieves. But the woman was so greedy that Zenkai grew disgusted. Finally he left her and journeyed far away to the province of Buzen, where he became a wandering mendicant.

To atone for his past, Zenkai resolved to accomplish some good deed in his lifetime. Knowing of a dangerous road over a cliff that had caused the death of many persons, he resolved to cut a tunnel through the mountain.

Begging food in the daytime, Zenkai worked at night digging his tunnel. When thirty years had gone by, the tunnel was 2,280 feet long, 20 feet high, and 30 feet wide.

Two years before the work was completed, the son of the official he had slain, who was a skillful swordsman, discovered where Zenaki was and set out to kill him in revenge.

"I will give you my life willingly," said Zenkai. "Only let me finish this work. When it is completed, then you may kill me."

So the son agreed to wait. Several months passed and Zenkai kept on digging. The son grew tired of doing nothing and began to help with the digging. After he had helped for more than a year, he came to admire Zenkai's strong will and character.

At last the tunnel was completed and the people could use it to travel in safety.

"Now cut off my head," said Zenkai. "My work is done."

"How can I cut off my own teacher's head?" asked the younger man with tears in his eyes.

Adapted from a traditional Zen story

Taking Time

Zi Qing was a maker of ornate wooden frames for hanging ceremonial bells and drums. Anyone who saw his work stood in awe of his superior craftsmanship. One day when Lord Yu came to Zi Qing's workshop and saw an example of his work, he said to him, "Zi Qing, where did you get the skill to fashion this frame of such incredible beauty?"

Zi Qing replied: "I am an ordinary carpenter and have no special skill. But I might mention just in passing how I prepare myself before I begin to carve the wood."

"Please do," said Lord Yu.

"First, I must fast in order to obtain an inner calm. After three days of fasting, my mind is still and I have laid aside any wish for personal gain. By the fifth day, I have become impervious to outside praise or criticism. After seven days, I enter a state of internal discipline and forget all about my own physical needs. At this stage even the command of the emperor cannot move me, and I am now ready for work. I go into the forest and search for a tree of natural beauty and perfection. Having found one, I cut it down. Finally, I sketch on a piece of paper a design for a frame, one that I have already conceived in my mind. Then, and only then, do I begin to carve the wood. I will not start if I have not taken all of these steps, for I know that only when I have integrated my own nature with the nature of the tree will it be possible to create a perfect frame."

Bishop John Tong,
from Zhuangzi, *adapted from a quotation in*
Challenges and Hopes: Stories from the Catholic Church in China
(Taipei: Wisdom Press, 1999)

Looking in One's Mirror

Wei Zheng was an extraordinary statesman of the early Tang dynasty. He often spoke bluntly to Emperor Taizong. After his death, the emperor sighed, "Using bronze as a mirror makes it easy to tidy ourselves up; using history as a mirror makes us clear about the cause of the rise and fall of dynasties; and using other people as a mirror makes us capable of weighing advantages and disadvantages. I often use the three mirrors to examine my faults. Now that Wei Zheng is dead, I have lost one mirror."

From Old History of the Tang Dynasty,
adapted from a quotation in Lo Wing Huen and Sun Li Jie,
Best Chinese Idioms, 3 *(Hong Kong: Hai Feng Publishing Co., 1997)*

A Golden Millet Dream

One day in the first year of Emperor Xuanzong's reign in the Tang dynasty, a young traveler spent the night at an inn in Handan in present-day Hebei. There he met Lu Weng, a Taoist priest. Though strangers, they immediately engaged in conversation. The young man was in low spirits, complaining that his present circumstances fell far short of his expectations. Lu Weng asked him to explain what he meant. The young man replied, "A man should do great things. He should become a general or a minister, and become rich and wealthy and enjoy all the privileges that life can offer. But so far I've gotten nowhere." As he finished speaking, he looked so tired that he seemed about to fall asleep.

The innkeeper was steaming millet as the two guests were talking. Upon hearing the young man's story, Lu Weng gave him a pillow. "Go to sleep on my pillow and your wishes will all come true." The young man took the pillow and fell asleep without even having bothered to take off his clothes. Soon he began to dream.

In his dream, he married the beautiful daughter of the wealthy Cui family and lived in luxury. The next year he passed the imperial examination and was given an office. Soon he was given a higher office, and then a higher office still. Further promotions followed, and eventually he became prime minister. However, his rise in position and power aroused the jealousy of other officials who falsely charged him with preparing to launch a coup. He was arrested and put in jail. In prison he lamented to his wife, "For years I sought power and money, but for what? I'd rather be wearing my jacket of coarse cloth and riding my little black horse along the road to Handan, going wherever I please." He was so overcome by grief that he considered committing suicide. Fortunately the emperor soon granted him a pardon, sending him into exile.

Many years later, the emperor realized that the charge against him had been false. He reappointed him prime minister, conferred even greater honors on him, and heaped him with gifts. His five sons and dozen grandsons became officials, garnering more power and honor. When they married girls from influential families, he was even happier. As he grew old, he rejoiced in his fertile lands, huge mansions, beautiful women, and fine horses. Thus he passed his life in great luxury and he was over eighty when he died.

At this point the young man suddenly woke up. He was still in the same inn, and Lu Weng was sitting beside him. The millet the innkeeper had prepared was still being cooked. In a sudden flash of understanding he achieved enlightenment.

Traditional story, Beatrice Liu Yanli, Handan (Hebei), China

The Wisdom of Allah

One day, as Nasreddin the Hoca was working in his little garden, he began to feel very warm. Seeing no one about, he slipped off his turban to cool his head a bit and then sat down in the pleasant shade of a walnut tree. Now, the Hoca's mind was seldom idle, and while he relaxed for a few minutes in the shade, he meditated upon the great wisdom of Allah. Chancing to find a watermelon in the garden, he smiled to himself.

"Now there," said he, "is something I'd have done differently had I been Allah. See that great, lovely watermelon growing on a spindly little vine, and then consider the walnut, a midget nut upon a great and lordly tree. Ah, who can fathom the wisdom of Allah? If I had been arranging matters, I should have given the walnuts to the puny vine, and reserved the watermelons for this magnificent tree." So musing, he nodded off.

While he was dozing, a walnut fell from the tree and landed with a substantial thump on the top of the Hoca's bald head. Suddenly awakened, Nasreddin the Hoca ruefully rubbed the lump that was beginning to swell on his scalp. Then an understanding smile spread over his face. In due reverence, he fell to his knees.

"O, Allah!" he murmured, "Forgive me my presumption. Thy wisdom is indeed great. Suppose I had been arranging matters? I should just now have been hit upon the head by a watermelon. Ah, Allah, great indeed is thy wisdom!"

Anonymous from Turkey,
adapted from a quotation in
Prayer without Borders: Celebrating Global Wisdom
(Catholic Relief Services, 2004)

Wisdom from India

It always pleased the master to hear people recognize their ignorance. "Wisdom tends to grow in proportion to one's awareness of one's ignorance," he claimed.

When asked for an explanation, he said, "When you come to see that you are not as wise today as you thought you were yesterday, you are wiser today."

William Dych, S.J., ed., Anthony de Mello
(Orbis Books, 1999)

Escape

The master became a legend in his lifetime. It is said that God once sought his advice: "I want to play a game of hide-and-seek with humankind. I asked my angels, 'Where is the best place to hide?' Some said the depths of the ocean. Others, the top of the highest mountain. Still others, the far side of the moon or a distant star. What do you suggest?"

Said the master, "Hide in the human heart. That's the last place they will think of!"

William Dych, S.J., ed., Anthony de Mello
(Orbis Books, 1999)

Respect for Elders

In Bangladesh a *fakir* (mendicant) is one who dispenses wisdom. People come to him for advice. It is spiritual counsel that is sought; the *fakir* does not pretend to have knowledge in matters material. Some *fakirs* can be recognized easily by the red clothing they wear. The red garb serves as an invitation for seekers to approach. The youths crowd close to a bearded, elderly wise man, having ears and eyes open wide to him, attentive to whatever shrewd comments he may offer them—such a sight warms the hearts of all adult Bengalis. They like to see their years respected; the *fakir* stands for all of them. Young people in this culture do, in general, listen to their elders. They may not always follow the advice offered to them, but they give their wise ones a hearing. No person is thought to be irrelevant merely by reason of his or her advanced age.

Observation, Father Bob McCahill, M.M., Bangladesh

Wisdom

It is better to develop wisdom within ourselves
Than to scrutinize and judge others.
It is better to master our own waywardness
Than to try to control other people.
If we are content with our own lives
We will avoid the frenzy of ambition.
The Way builds a life
That never will die.

English translation by Joseph Petulla
The Tao Te Ching and the Christian Way
(Orbis Books, 1998)

Confucius on Wisdom

Confucius lived a life filled with enthusiasm for learning. Although he was just a poor young man in the country of Lu, he earned the respect of many people because of his politeness and love for learning. Aside from studying different things, Confucius spent many years serving in public offices as an advisor and minister. During the last few years of his life, he was again offered a public position, which he declined. Instead, he spent the remaining years of his life teaching and writing. Confucius died at the age of seventy-two.

Confucius said, "To know what you know and know what you don't know is the characteristic of one who knows."

Confucius said, "A man who has made a mistake and doesn't correct it is making another mistake."

Confucius said, "A man who has a beautiful soul always has beautiful things to say, but a man who says beautiful things does not necessarily have a beautiful soul."

Confucius said, "The superior man understands what is right, the inferior man understands what will sell."

Confucius said, "The superior man loves his soul; the inferior man loves his property. The superior man always remembers how he was punished for his mistakes; the inferior man always remembers the gift he received."

Confucius said, "The superior man blames himself; the inferior man blames others."

Adapted from Linking the World through English II
(Philippines: Diwa Scholastic Press, 2006)

The Legend of the Acagui Seed

There is an exotic fruit known as the *acagui*, also called the *anacardio*, which has the shape of a little bell. Unlike other fruits the *acagui*, yellow and sweet when ripe, has its seed on the outside of its shell.

According to one Filipino legend, there was once in the forest a great feast to which all the animals were invited. The seed in an *acagui* heard all the sounds of merriment. It could only sigh, "Oh, if only I could get out of my dark house to see the party!"

A fairy on her way to the festival heard the seed's voice as it called out to her, "Gentle and gracious fairy, do let me get out of my house of pulp so that I, too, can see the fun."

The fairy took pity on the seed and with her delicate magic wand she touched the *acagui*. The seed slid out and appeared on the surface.

The black seed remarked in awe, "Oh, how astonishing is this world! What a wonderful experience it is to contemplate this lovely scenery! Oh good and beautiful fairy, don't make me go back inside the fruit, don't make me go inside again where only darkness and solitude are my companions! I feel so happy here."

The festivities went on until all the animals returned to their homes. Silence reigned once more. Then the wind began to blow violently, accompanied by a heavy downpour of rain beating down anything that lay in its path. The little seed shuddered with every flash of thunder and lightning. The poor thing tried to communicate with the fairy, pleading, "Listen to me once more, dear fairy! Do listen to me! Let me go back inside the fruit where I can be safe from the rapping of the rain and the alarming sound of lightning and thunder."

The seed's begging turned to sobs, but they were all in vain. The fairy had disappeared forever. The seed of the *acagui*, since that time on, can be found attached to the shell of the fruit, a prey to all inclement weather.

> "O Lord, give me the grace to be content
> with what you give to me.
> No! More than that,
> let me rejoice in all you send me!"

Folk tale, Father Eugene F. Thalman, M.M., Hong Kong

Judge Not by Appearances

Zai Yu, a disciple of Confucius, had a smooth and eloquent tongue, which helped him win the favor of Confucius. As time went by, his laziness and moral failings were exposed. Confucius was then disgusted with him and said that he was hopeless.

Zi Yu was also one of Confucius's disciples. His extreme ugliness made Confucius dislike him. But Zi Yu was of good moral character and fine scholarship, and he judged things fairly. Later, when he traveled to teach in the various states, many disciples gathered to follow him and he gradually gained a high reputation. Knowing this, Confucius said with deep feeling, "I've overestimated Zai Yu by his words, and underestimated Zi Yu by his appearance."

From Records of the Historian,
adapted from a quotation in Lo Wing Huen and Sun Li Jie,
Best Chinese Idioms, 3 *(Hong Kong: Hai Feng Publishing Co., 1997)*

Desire Less

"How would spirituality help a man of the world like me?" asked the businessman.

"It would help you to have more," said the master.

"How?"

"By teaching you to desire less."

William Dych, S.J., ed., Anthony de Mello
(*Orbis Books, 1999*)

The True Wealth

Happy are those who find wisdom,
    and those who get understanding,
for her income is better than silver,
    and her revenue better than gold.
She is more precious than jewels,
    and nothing you desire can compare with her.
Long life is in her right hand;
    in her left hand are riches and honor.
Her ways are ways of pleasantness,
    and all her paths are peace.
She is a tree of life to those who lay hold of her;
    those who hold her fast are called happy.

Proverbs 3:13–18 (NRSV)

One God— Many Faith Traditions

Lead me from the unreal to the real.
Lead me from darkness to light.
Lead me from death to immortality.
Upanishads

The spirituality of Asian peoples manifests itself in many traditions. Around 85 percent of the world's adherents of religions other than Christianity are found in Asia. Buddhism and Hinduism have hundreds of millions of faithful, and Muslims in Asia are seven times more numerous than Christians, who make up less than three percent of the population.

While there are incidents of religious tension and misunderstanding, genuine friendship and appreciation dominate relations among the followers of the living faiths in most Asian nations. All profit from a reverential respect of the "other" that comes from seeing the other's values in practice and from observing how spiritual experiences, contemplation, and prayer spring from faith.

Renewal movements within Asia's faith traditions have engendered a spirit of authentic dialogue and a common desire to serve the millions of Asia's poor and needy. While the percentage of adherents of the various Asian faith traditions will probably not alter significantly in the near future, all are called to reverence the one God revealed in Asia's many faiths. As you read these stories, ask yourself: In which of these stories do I find genuine faith?

Harmony Prayer

O Lord, I cry for peace.
Purify my eyes to see peace,
Purify my mind to understand peace,
Purify my heart to love peace,
Purify my memory to work for peace,
The peace that comes from you,
Love and compassion.

O Lord, sustain my vision of peace
Following your inspiration.
You have many ways of revealing your
Presence and love for humanity,
But your style is constant:
You are in dialogue with all,
You care for all.

Make me, O Lord, a sign of your peace,
Living a life in dialogue with you
To understand your silence
And seek your presence;
In dialogue with myself
To rediscover the meaning of my life;
In dialogue with others
To move together in harmony with all;
And, in dialogue with creation
To care for the earth.

Give me, O Lord,
The courage to live in dialogue
In the midst of divisions and conflicts
And to build peace with all people
Of sincere hearts who believe
In your love and compassion.
Amen.

Silsilah Dialogue Movement,
Father James H. Kroeger, M.M., Manila, Philippines

Forgiveness in Bangladesh

My landlord and Bangladeshi father, as he used to call himself, is one of the clearest examples of how God is present in all of us. About two years before Kashem Ali died, he sent a message to my little hut that he wanted to see me. I knew his health was not good. He was suffering from a weak heart and the medicine he was taking was not very effective.

When I arrived in the dark, gloomy room, I found him covered with quilts to keep him warm. I bent over him and heard him say in a gravelly voice, "I am going to die." My helpless reply was, "We all have to die someday."

He continued on, leaving me awestruck: "I want to ask your forgiveness for anything I have done against you."

I did not know how to respond. It was a time for *my* tears, but, as usual, they did not fall. Still, my heart was in my throat. Having heard thousands of confessions during my ministry in the Philippines, I was now hearing one of the most sincere, unaffected confessions I've ever heard. All I could utter in reply was, "You haven't done anything to offend me, but, as you request, I do forgive anything you may think you did against me." I asked God in my heart to forgive this good man.

Although he lived for another two years, much of the time in pain and weakness, I could only admire the man for his integrity. Even now, because of him, the lines in my former religious education that seemed to divide religions have fallen from my heart.

Father Doug Venne, M.M., Dhaka, Bangladesh

Ninety-Nine Names for God

Lejla Demiri is a Muslim woman studying Christian theology at the Gregorian University in Rome.

"As a Muslim, thinking about peace and religion, I am always reminded of the meaning of the word 'Islam.' The word means 'submission to God' and it comes from the Arabic root s-l-m, which means 'peace.'

"Moreover, *Salam*, peace, is one of the ninety-nine names of God in the Muslim tradition. All Muslims end their five daily prayers with this short prayer: 'Oh God, You are peace, and from You comes peace.'

"Additionally, in one of his sayings the Prophet Muhammad points out that 'You will not enter heaven unless you believe, and you will not become true believers unless you love each other.'"

Adapted from Zenit News Agency (Rome)

Generawi

Generawi worked as a nurse many years ago in a Malaysian hospital that specialized in treating leprosy patients. He had a good friend whose three sons he regarded almost as his own, since he himself was not married. The boys grew fond of their "uncle" who would regale them with stories and little gifts.

One day, the friend died rather suddenly of a heart attack, leaving behind a distraught widow and three young boys. Without a second thought, Generawi took it upon himself to support his extended family despite his meager earnings. After some time, he decided that it would be more appropriate for him to move in with the widow so that the boys would grow up with a father. But this would mean that he would have to marry the widow and here was a problem: he was a staunch Muslim and the boys and their mother were Roman Catholics.

Now, Muslims, very much like Catholics, are obliged to bring up their children in the faith they themselves profess. Would the widow and the boys be willing to convert? There were also practical considerations. For example, he did not eat pork, while the widow and her boys habitually did. How could they live together under one roof?

Generawi made a decision. He would let things be as they were. After marrying the widow and moving in, he kept a separate kitchen and asked his wife, who was older than he by a number of years, to cook him Muslim meals. And so the new family lived on.

The boys grew up, married and started their own families. They never forgot Generawi's kindness and sacrifice and although they never got over calling him "Uncle," their children grew up calling him "Kong Kong" or "grandfather." Years later, the widow died, and, in his early sixties, Generawi decided to re-marry, this time a Muslim convert who bore him four children. A retiree now, Generawi immersed himself in religion.

He prayed five times daily and taught himself and his own children to read the Qu'ran. No stranger to Roman Catholicism, he also studied the Bible, drawing comparisons with Islam. Even as he covered the doors of his house with hand-written Islamic calligraphy and saved money to make the obligatory pilgrimage to Mecca, Generawi gave his Catholic grandchildren Bibles for their birthdays. Open-minded and generous, he was only too happy to enter into religious dialogue with them, but they shied away, conscious that their own knowledge of Christianity paled in comparison to that of their Kong Kong.

In our world today, where the divide between Christianity and Islam becomes increasingly pronounced, individuals like Generawi stand out. He saw people not as Muslims or Christians or Buddhists but as human beings who believed in one and the same almighty God. We talk often about interreligious dialogue. Here that dialogue is personified. I'm very proud of my grandfather Generawi.

Alvin Frederick Ng, S.J., Kuching, Malaysia, studying in Manila

The Fallout of the Iraq War in Bangladesh

I was in Bangladesh in the spring of 2003 when the United States began the attack on Iraq. Muslim friends warned me not to leave our seminary compound unescorted. It was reported that some twelve hundred Bangladeshis had gone to the Iraqi Embassy in Dhaka to volunteer to go to Iraq as suicide bombers. When I finally took the bus to Dhaka, I saw many effigies of President Bush hanging along the route.

A week into the war, one of our young seminarians, Sujatta, became ill. As his temperature rose to 105 we suspected cerebral malaria. On Friday morning, his mother, two other seminarians, and I took Sujatta by ambulance to a teaching hospital twenty-five miles away. Because there were no beds available, we laid Sujatta on a mat on the floor at the foot of one of the beds. The bed was occupied by a teenage Muslim boy with a tumor on his neck. His father, a devout Muslim and loving father, stayed with his son.

In Bangladesh it is the responsibility of patients' relatives to provide for their needs. In our rush to get to the hospital, we had brought nothing with us, but the other patients and their relatives offered us drinking water and we shared their grief when family members died that afternoon.

That same Friday afternoon the father of the boy with the neck tumor was able to take his son to the mosque for the *Jumma* prayer. (I'm sure America was excoriated in that day's sermon). Before leaving for the mosque, the father promised to pray for Sujatta, and he invited me to rest on his son's bed during their absence.

Happily, Sujatta recovered, and after two and a half days the doctors released him. When I asked the doctors for the bill, they replied, "There is no bill! We will not accept a *taka* from you! *Asalaam O'Aleikum*! (Peace be with you!) *Allah Hafez*! (God bless you!)"

It has been my constant experience during these twenty-five years in Bangladesh that if Muslims feel you share their basic faith and values and see that you are "in a sense in the same boat" with them, a marvelous experience of oneness and God-inspired solidarity results!

True story, Father Bill McIntire, M.M., Bangladesh

Basic Family Values

Tasneem was a young Catholic man living at home in predominantly Muslim Pakistan. When his mother suggested that it was time he get married, he agreed, and his mother and the matchmakers began their search for a suitable wife.

A young Catholic woman, Asma, a schoolteacher, was found, and Tasneem went to visit her at her school. They talked for twenty minutes, felt comfortable with each other, and ten days later they were married with all the traditional Pakistani and Catholic rites.

Then, a week later, they moved to Cambodia. Neither of them had been out of Pakistan before, but Tasneem felt constrained by limited opportunities and religious discrimination at home, so he decided to seek a different life elsewhere.

Meeting a prospective husband or wife, marrying, and moving to a new country, all in the space of three weeks, would seem incomprehensible to most North Americans or Europeans, but the traditional values of many Asian countries make such undertakings not only possible but successful.

Perhaps Asian people understand the meaning of love better than many Westerners, who tend to focus on feelings of love. Many Asians would see love as a choice rather than a feeling. They know that there will be difficulties and disagreements in marriage, but they commit themselves to making it work, and they are supported by strong familial and societal values. They know that real love comes through living out a commitment and making choices together.

Tasneem and Asma are a perfect example of this committed love, which they still exemplify in Cambodia with their two lovely daughters.

True story, Father Charles Dittmeier, Phnom Penh, Cambodia

Seeds of God in Asian Soil

*"Faith is the bird that feels the light
and sings when the dawn is still dark."*
R. Tagore

Asians are genuinely comfortable being people of faith. In Asia, external signs of religious conviction meet one at every turn. Temples abound in Thailand. Small chapels dot the countryside as well as city streets in the Philippines. Red crosses light up the night sky of Korean cities. Torii, Japanese gateways designating holy ground, the gateway between the physical and spiritual worlds, can be found throughout Japan. In Asia, Muslim, Buddhist, and Christian believers commonly wear religious garb or symbols in public places. Buses and taxis display sacred images, prayer beads, and quotes from sacred scriptures.

Such external manifestations of religious belief spring from deeply held convictions. People love their faith and they want others to appreciate this fact. For most of Asia's four billion people there is no apparent dichotomy between faith and life.

Visible displays reflect interior dispositions. Although God remains a mystery, greater than any creed, ritual, or place of worship, God also is very real to people and can be found in the ordinariness of life, in deeds of neighborly service, in meditation, in public and private prayers. Since God permeates all of life in Asia, anyone who claims to have faith must manifest it in holiness of life.

Gandhi noted that any faith-witnessing or preaching in Asia should imitate the rose:

"A rose does not need to preach. It simply spreads its fragrance. The fragrance is its own sermon. . . . The fragrance of religious and spiritual life is much finer and subtler than that of the rose."

Enjoy the fragrance of Asia.

So Sorry

When the Japanese attacked the Philippines in 1941, they interned the Americans there, including nuns from the Maryknoll community. Food was scarce, but the sisters noticed that the Japanese officer in charge always shared the little food they had equally among the soldiers and the prisoners.

The sisters placed a crucifix in one corner of their quarters and they would gather there to pray each day. As Christmas approached, the sisters gathered scraps of bamboo, cloth and wood, and constructed a crib scene. From the wood they carved figurines of Mary, Joseph, the shepherds, the animals, and the baby Jesus. On Christmas Eve they placed the infant Jesus in the crib. When the Japanese officer saw the infant in the crib, he pointed at the crucifix, "Is that the same person?"

The sisters said, "Yes, that's the same person." And the Japanese officer replied, "I am so sorry."

True story, a Maryknoll Sister, the Philippines

Butter in the Milk

One day a young aspirant went to see an old saint who lived in a little hut beside a river. The atmosphere of the simple hut calmed the aspirant's mind and he enjoyed the company of the saint very much.

When the time came to leave, the young man asked the saint if he could ask him an important question.

"Of course, my son," said the saint.

"Where can I find God?"

The saint smiled. "That is not an easy question. Allow me to dwell on it. Come again tomorrow and I will answer it. Also, please bring a glass of milk."

The young man agreed and went home, excited that the next day his question would be answered. He thought it odd that the saint had requested a glass of milk, but it was a simple request, so the next day he returned with the glass of milk.

The saint thanked him for the milk and poured it into his begging bowl. Then he put his fingers in the milk and lifted them up, but when the milk ran through them he frowned and repeated the gesture, with the same result.

Perplexed, the young man watched. He wished the saint would finish with his foolishness and get to the question the young man had asked.

The saint began feeling through the milk with his hand, occasionally lifting his hand out and staring at his palm, but when he saw his palm was empty he would return to fishing through the milk.

At last the young man's patience was exhausted and he said, "Guruji, what are you looking for?"

"I have heard that there is butter in milk," said the saint. "I am searching for the butter."

Before he could stop himself, the young man laughed. "It is not like that. The butter is not separate from the milk, it is a part of it. You have to convert the milk to yogurt and then churn it to make the butter come out."

"Very good!" said the saint. "I believe you have the answer to your question." And he quaffed the bowl of milk in one long drink. "Now go and churn the milk of your soul until you have found God."

Anonymous from India,
adapted from Prayer without Borders: Celebrating Global Wisdom
(Catholic Relief Services, 2004)

What Did Jesus Do for Fun?

A priest worked for many years with the Atayal, one of the native peoples of Taiwan. The Atayal have their own distinct language and cultural heritage. By drawing on their culture, in which no event can be celebrated without a meal, the priest summarized the teaching of the Christian faith in four sets of questions and answers.

Question 1: When Jesus came to live among us, what did he do?

Answer 1: According to the gospels, he participated in a lot of meals.

Question 2: What was Jesus' message?

Answer 2: His message was to invite people to banquets.

Question 3: What must followers of Jesus do?

Answer 3: They should have meals together.

Question 4: What else must the followers of Jesus do?

Answer 4: They should invite others to meals, especially the poor.

True story, Father Dick Devoe, M.M., Taiwan

Forgiveness Papers

The Taoist teacher, Chang Tao-ling, taught contrition, confession, and penance for one's sins. This was done by writing the name of the offended person on three pieces of paper. One piece of paper was put on a mountain for heaven. One piece was buried in the earth. And the third piece was thrown into the water.

Sin reaches to the heavens. Sin is to be buried. And from the waters of contrition, new life will come.

From a manuscript by Yves Raguin, S.J., Taoism and Taoist Religion
(Taipei: Ricci Institute of Chinese Studies, 1979)

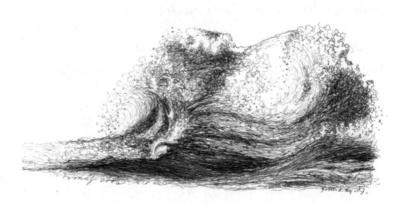

I Will Ask Allah

Word spread very quickly. I had received an emergency phone call in the early morning informing me that my younger sister in the States had been in a serious automobile accident involving a truck. Her injuries were life-threatening and the next forty-eight hours would be critical.

I immediately told the sad news to my fellow faculty members at the seminary in Davao in the southern Philippines. It wasn't long before everyone—including the kitchen staff—had heard the news.

When I finished teaching my two morning classes, I was surprised to see Utol waiting for me outside the classroom. Well known to all, Utol served as our "fish-supplier," personally delivering quality fresh fish three times a week.

Utol lived in a small Muslim coastal village near the seminary. In the early morning, he would collect the evening catch from his Muslim neighbors and distribute the fish to several regular customers, including the seminary.

Utol may have finished only one or two grades of school and couldn't read or write well. After years of laboring in the tropical sun, his complexion was very dark. Too poor to afford a dentist, he was missing several teeth. His hands were callused and scarred from years of fishing.

Utol began speaking in Cebuano, the local language. "The cooks in the kitchen told me what happened to your sister. I am so sorry to hear the sad news."

"Thank you very much for your concern and expression of sympathy," I replied. "You are very thoughtful; you waited for me for nearly two hours. You should be at home sleeping, as I'm sure you were up all night fishing."

Utol continued, "I want to tell you that I will pray to Allah for your sister's recovery. Allah will help her, I am sure."

"Thank you. Thank you," I said, holding back my tears.

As Utol turned to go, he assured me, "With Allah, all will be OK."

I was deeply moved. What faith! What trust in divine providence! What beautiful words, coming from the mouth of a man who obviously prays!

And my younger sister is still alive, thirty years later.

True story, Father James H. Kroeger, M.M., Manila, Philippines

Parable of the Whisperer

There was once a very old Chinese catechist in a certain diocese in China. Since there were no priests available, the bishop had no choice but to make use of this ninety-one-year-old catechist. Each Sunday the catechist organized a liturgy of the word and prayer service. He had lost his voice and could only whisper, so he was unable to preach. Instead, after someone read the gospel, everyone sat down for ten minutes in small groups to discuss what they heard. Some folks were uncomfortable and perspiring. Everyone was thinking hard about the gospel passage.

Did I mention that each Sunday the catechist chose the same verses from the Gospel of Matthew, the account of the last judgment (Matthew 25:31–46), in which people are separated into sheep (heading to heaven) and goats (heading to hell)?

What was the catechist's secret? He stood at the entrance of the church and whispered several questions to each Christian who entered. Based on the response, he directed each person to sit on either the right or the left side of the church.

These were his questions:

Did you give Jesus something to eat last week?

Did you comfort Jesus when he was sick last week?

Did you welcome Jesus the stranger last week?

If someone told the catechist that he or she didn't once see Jesus hungry, thirsty, a stranger, sick, or in prison all last week, then the catechist would whisper, "You dummy, Jesus was wearing disguises. Go sit on the left with the goats!"

During the discussion after the reading of the gospel, those sitting on the "goat side" planned what they had to do for

Jesus during the coming week so that on the following Sunday they could once again sit with the sheep. And the "sheep Christians" also had to plan so that on the following Sunday they wouldn't wind up with the goats.

Father Eugene F. Thalman, M.M., Hong Kong

Crossing the Border

It is only about 160 miles (as the crow flies), or a thirty-five-minute flight, from Dhaka, Bangladesh, to Kolkata (formerly Calcutta), India. But making the trip by road is a journey of about twelve hours, since one must take a ferry across the mighty Padma River and cross a sometimes tense Bangladesh-India border at Benapole.

Once when I was crossing this border, the Muslim officer-in-charge on the Bangladeshi side sternly asked me to enter his office. I did so with considerable apprehension, thinking that perhaps I was going to be harassed or barred from crossing or perhaps asked for a bribe.

The Muslim official, recognizing me as a foreign Christian, astonished me by shaking my hand and saying, "I am exceedingly grateful to Allah and to all of you that when my wife recently gave birth to our first-born son at Fatima (Catholic) Hospital in Jessore, she received truly excellent care at a relatively low price. How happy we are to accept Allah's gift of a healthy and beautiful son!"

The official, now my new friend, then showed me what lay under the glass on his desk, a Bengali translation of the Peace Prayer of Saint Francis of Assisi: "Make me a channel of your peace! Where there is hatred, let me sow your love! Where there is injury, your pardon, Lord! And where there's doubt, true faith in you!" We shook hands again and without any further difficulty I crossed the border that day and headed for Kolkata with a song in my heart!

True story, Father Bill McIntire, M.M., Mymensingh, Bangladesh

Respect for Prayer

Several men were going about their work when the call to afternoon prayer sounded from the minaret of the nearby mosque. One of them, a carpenter, put down his hammer and moved to a well operated by a hand-pump in order to perform ablutions in preparation for ritual prayer. Other men continued on their way, engrossed by the tasks at hand. Meanwhile, the carpenter looked around to find a suitably clean place for offering prayer, found it, and mounted a small table alongside the busy street. The table's owner was unknown to him. Quickly he positioned himself on it, closed his eyes, and fell into prayer. One or two other men glanced his way but did not follow his example. They approve of prayer wherever it takes place, and whenever. Neither they nor the carpenter thinks critically of the other. That is, the carpenter thought no ill of the others for missing prayer, nor did the others accuse the carpenter in their hearts for showing off his piety in a public place. For ritual prayer is good, they all admit, and helpful for all—even for those Muslims who, for whatever reason, fail to join in it.

Observation, Father Bob McCahill, M.M., Bangladesh

Prayer for Peace

I offer you peace.
I offer you love.
I offer you friendship.
I see your beauty.
I hear your need.
I feel your feelings.
My wisdom flows from the Highest Source.
I salute that Source in you.
Let us work together for unity and love.

Mahatma Gandhi,
Father James H. Kroeger, M.M.,
Manila, Philippines

Another Item on Santa's Wish List

I serve the HIV patients residing at the Wat Prabaat Buddhist Temple in Lopburi, Thailand. The temple cares for 250 AIDS patients. Although all the patients are of the Buddhist tradition, nonetheless they have heard about Santa, who brings joy and gifts. I was chosen by the staff to wear the Santa Claus suit and to "Ho, ho, ho." The smiles were radiant. We wanted each patient to know how special he or she was and we gave a bit of chocolate to each one.

When we came to Nalong, a thirty-two-year-old Thai man who is an artist, he invited Santa to sit on his bed so that he could ask Santa something. "Is it true," he asked, "that Santa Claus can grant any wish you ask of him?"

I replied, "It is true that Santa wants to help everyone."

Nalong put his hand on Santa's bulging stomach made of pillows and spoke softly, "Then all I want is to be cured of AIDS." At that moment I was so touched by what he said that I couldn't speak. After a short silence, I looked at him and said, "It is not only the hope of Santa Claus, but of everyone in the world, that a cure for AIDS will be found soon.* Therefore, we do not give up hope, but we live each day in the hope for that day to come soon." Nalong smiled, and as I handed him the chocolate, we saw in each other's eyes the gratitude and joy that came from sharing that special moment together.

Father Mike Bassano, M.M., Lopburi, Thailand

*In 2003, 58,000 people in Thailand died of AIDS.

Different Faiths Live Together

One important event in my life happened in a village in Bangladesh where I live and work with the people.

A number of years ago I met Rahim, a fifteen-year-old boy. We worked together in the fields and became good friends. He was very kind to me, whereas some of the other lads his age mocked me as a foreigner.

After contracting some kind of infection in his lungs, Rahim died several days later. To show my fondness for him, I offered to work with his father for a year.

His father accepted my offer and so I went to work each day from early in the morning until late afternoon. When possible, I did whatever Masum Ali asked me. Since I worked for the family, they fed me at noon.

Masum Ali's youngest daughter, Asheda, sometimes slept on my shoulder in the afternoons. Since he and I both had beards, she used to call both of us "Abba."

One day Aleya, the eldest daughter, said to me, "Your country pays your support, doesn't it?"

"Who told you that?"

"Oh, that's what I heard," was her reply.

"No, I don't get any funds from my government. My family and friends send me help for my food, clothing, and shelter because they believe that what I am doing is good."

At that moment, some birds flew down and started to peck away at the rice drying in the farmyard. It made me think of the words of Jesus when he spoke about how God feeds the birds. I continued, "Aleya, do you see those birds? Who feeds them?"

Her answer was immediate: "Allah feeds them."

"Yes, but Allah takes better care of us than the birds."

I was sitting outside their hut and heard her mother, who was inside, call out, "You are a man of wisdom." Although she had never had any schooling or even been to the town that was only five miles away, she recognized the truth of what I had said.

Indeed, the Spirit of the One God is present in all people.

Father Doug Venne, M.M., Dhaka, Bangladesh

Between Friends

Abdul the blacksmith, Ali the farmer, and Karim the imam lived in the same village. Abdul was a drunkard and, despite his claim that he was a blacksmith, had never done an honest day's work in his life. Ali was a God-fearing man who toiled diligently on his farm from sunrise to sunset. Although inclined to fits of temper and occasional brawls, he was nevertheless a good and upright man. Karim, the village imam, was so holy that people who suffered from depression would come from miles around to gaze at his radiant face and be cured.

By a strange twist of fate, these three men found themselves afflicted with leprosy. In accordance with the strict laws of the land, they were compelled to leave their families for fear of spreading their terrible disease. A small hut was hastily put up for them on the outskirts of the village and all three moved there, settling in as best they could.

One night the three of them had a similar dream in which they each heard the voice of God telling them, "Pray for healing." Upon waking, when they realized that they had dreamt exactly the same thing, they concluded that their dream must have really been sent by God. So they began to pray earnestly for a miraculous healing.

After three days, Abdul the drunkard was healed. He returned to the village at once, convinced that for some reason he was dearer to God than his two companions.

After three months, Ali the farmer was also healed. He also resumed his life in the village, puzzled as to why he would be dearer to God than the imam, who was still very much a leper. "I suppose," mused the farmer on his way home, "that the imam's reputation of holiness may be a sham. If he were really that holy, he would have been cured before the two of us." Yet why had the drunkard been healed so quickly? Why did he himself, an upright man, have to wait three months for his cure while that ne'er-do-well had been cured after only three days?

Many years passed. Karim the imam continued to pray for healing but remained a leper. No one came anymore to look on his face and his little hut was carefully avoided. Besides, his face and body had become a frightful sight.

Ali continued to ponder these things while he went about his work.

One night Ali heard God's voice addressing him in a dream: "Ali, my son, I know that your heart is troubled over the fate of Karim the imam. You are wondering why, on the one hand, a worse man than you was cured before you, and why, on the other hand, a better man than you is still a leper. Listen and you will understand."

God's voice continued, "I answered Abdul's prayer quickly because of his great weakness. Three days of trust were all he was capable of. If I had delayed granting his request he would have fallen into despair. In your case I delayed three months because you had a greater trust in me. But after three months you would have lost heart. Do you understand?"

The farmer answered, "Yes, Lord, I understand. And I agree with everything you have said. But now, what about Karim the imam? Will he be cured one day or will his prayer go forever unheard?"

A long silence followed. Then finally the voice spoke again, this time with a hint of weariness. "Because the imam's faith is total, I can let his prayer go unheard. You see, the imam is my friend and knows my heart. Whether I answer his prayer or not, he trusts in me. In fact, the longer I delay, the deeper his trust grows. And now his closeness to me has become so great that it no longer matters to him whether I heal him or not. I have become everything to him."

When Ali woke the next morning, he could still hear those words ringing in his heart, "I have become everything to him."

From his bed he looked through the window toward the rising sun. "Will there ever be a day when God is everything to me?" he wondered. Then he looked at his strong and healthy hands. And, for the first time in his life, he regretted that he was not a leper.

Adapted from Greater Than Our Hearts, *by Nil Guillemette*
(Manila: St. Paul Publications, 1988)

List of Stories

Of Related Interest

Joseph G. Healey

Once Upon a Time in Africa
Stories of Wisdom and Joy
ISBN 1-57075-527-2

"Once Upon a Time is packed with the 'wisdom and joy'
of the African people. It is a wonderful introduction not only
to their faith life but to how they somehow manage to 'keep
on keeping; on' despite all that imperils life and ravages
their beautiful continent and its people.
Once you start reading, you can't put it down. . . ."
Diana L. Hayes, Georgetown University

Please support your local bookstore, or call 1-800-258-5838.
For a free catalogue, please write us at
Orbis Books, Box 308
Maryknoll NY 10545-0308
or visit our website at www.orbisbooks.com

Thank you for reading *Once Upon a Time in Asia: Stories of Harmony
and Peace.*
We hope you enjoyed it.